ABSOLUTELY AMAZING
STRESS RELIEVING
WILD ANIMALS

ISBN-13: 978-1546763604
ISBN-10: 1546763600

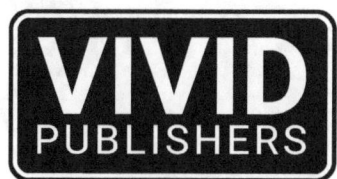

ABSOLUTELY AMAZING
STRESS RELIEVING
WILD ANIMALS

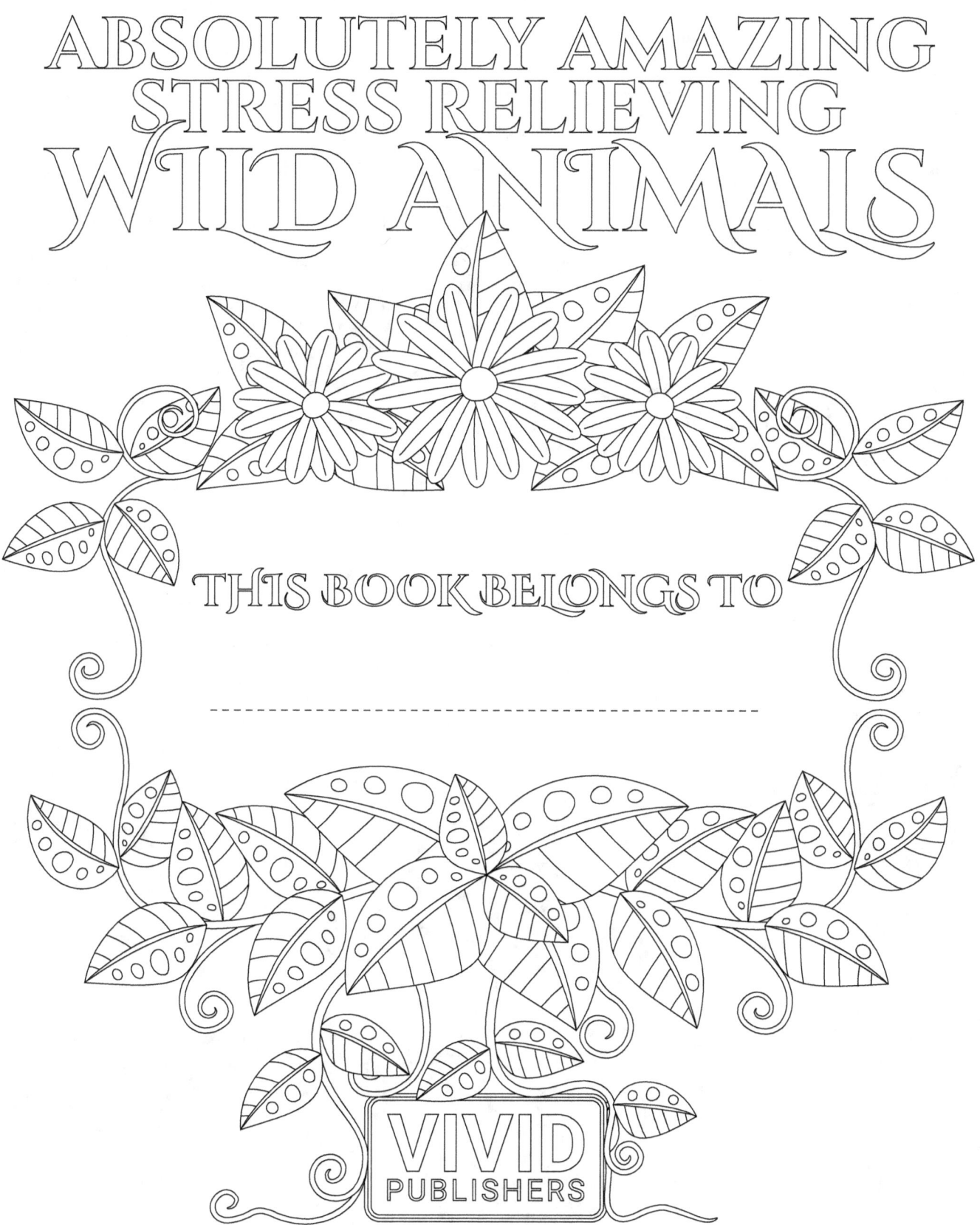

THIS BOOK BELONGS TO

VIVID
PUBLISHERS

INTRODUCTION

Thank you for purchasing our very first title "Absolutely Amazing, Stress Relieving, Wild Animals".

This is a labor of love that we've been working on passionately for a long time & are proud to present to you the final outcome.

All drawings have been hand drawn in a combination of realism & intricate patterning and digitized to create line art that is crisp, clean and optimized for coloring.

We would certainly like to hear your feedback & suggestions for future releases of which you can stay up to date through our social media pages.

Here's to vivid coloring & a stress free happy life!

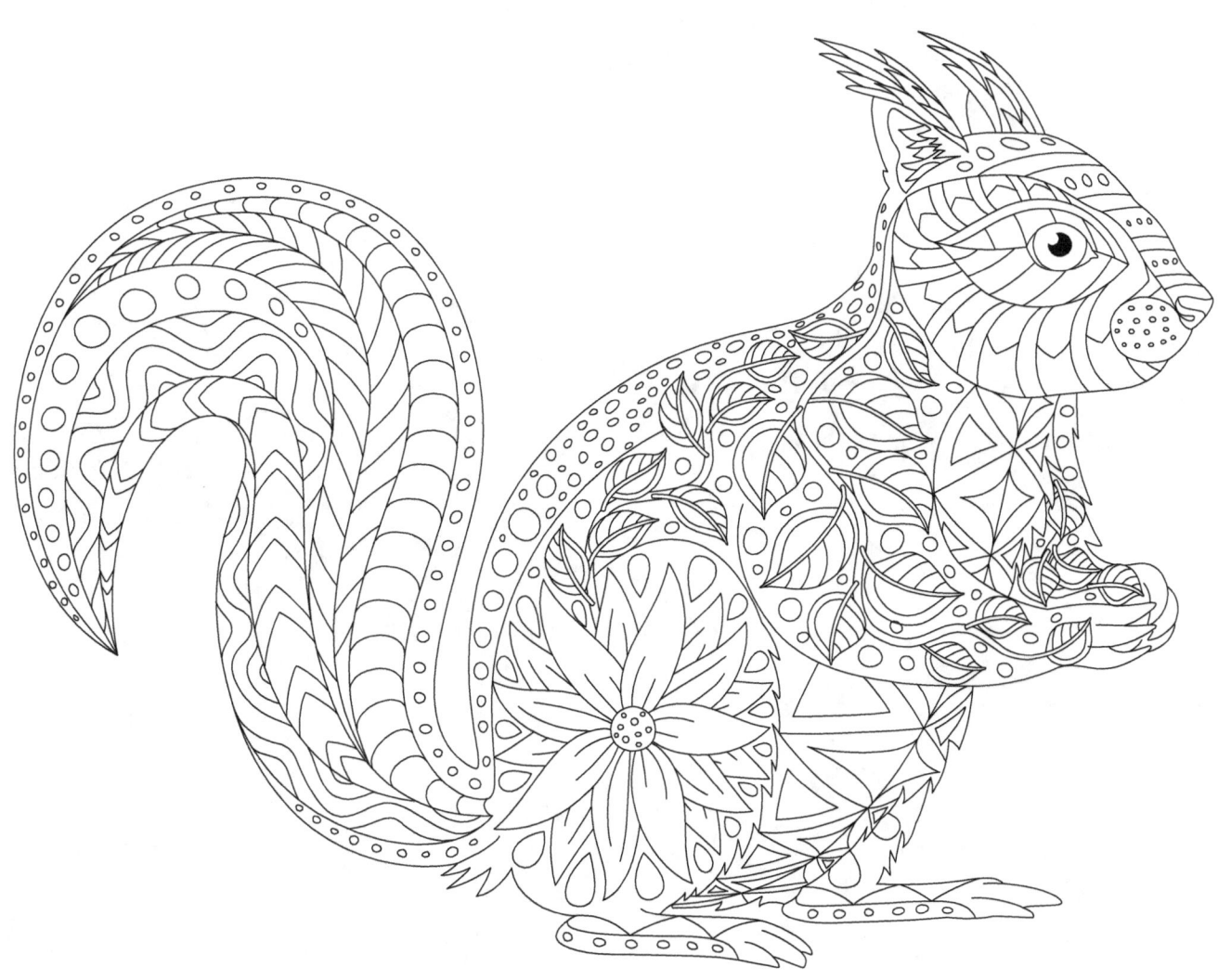

HOW TO USE

This is pretty simple. First up- would be a good idea to switch off your electronics, including the smart phone (we can get back to it, to share the awesome work you have completed later on!).

Got your favorite coloring medium ready? Great! Now, just choose any animal that catches your eye from the jungle of 40 designs & get started.

One thing is for sure - once you complete the page, you would be proud of a job well done and in the process be a much more relaxed person.

If at any time you feel like not coloring, it's best to stop and move on to other things.

You can use any medium from crayons to pencils & markers, as long as they have a fine tip, as the illustrations can get quite detailed.

A note on the use of markers: *Even though the illustrations are printed one per page, to give additional protection please place a thick paper or cardboard beneath the page you are coloring so that the ink will not bleed through to the next page.*

Tip for complex pages: *For illustrations with entwined plants, it would be good to first color them in, so that you are left with the wild animals in clear view.*

I think we've covered it all. **Happy coloring!**

SHARE YOUR ART

We would love to see how you bring these pages to life. *Get your art out of the wilderness & share it with the world!*

Reach out to us at:

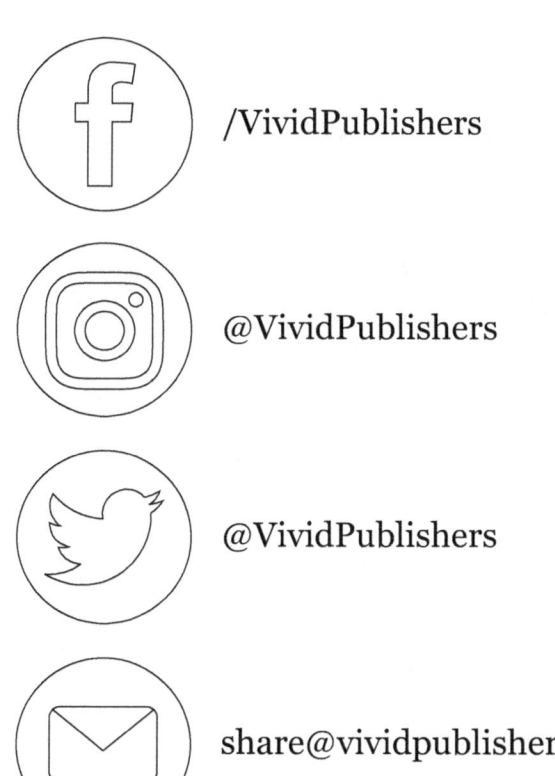

/VividPublishers

@VividPublishers

@VividPublishers

share@vividpublishers.com

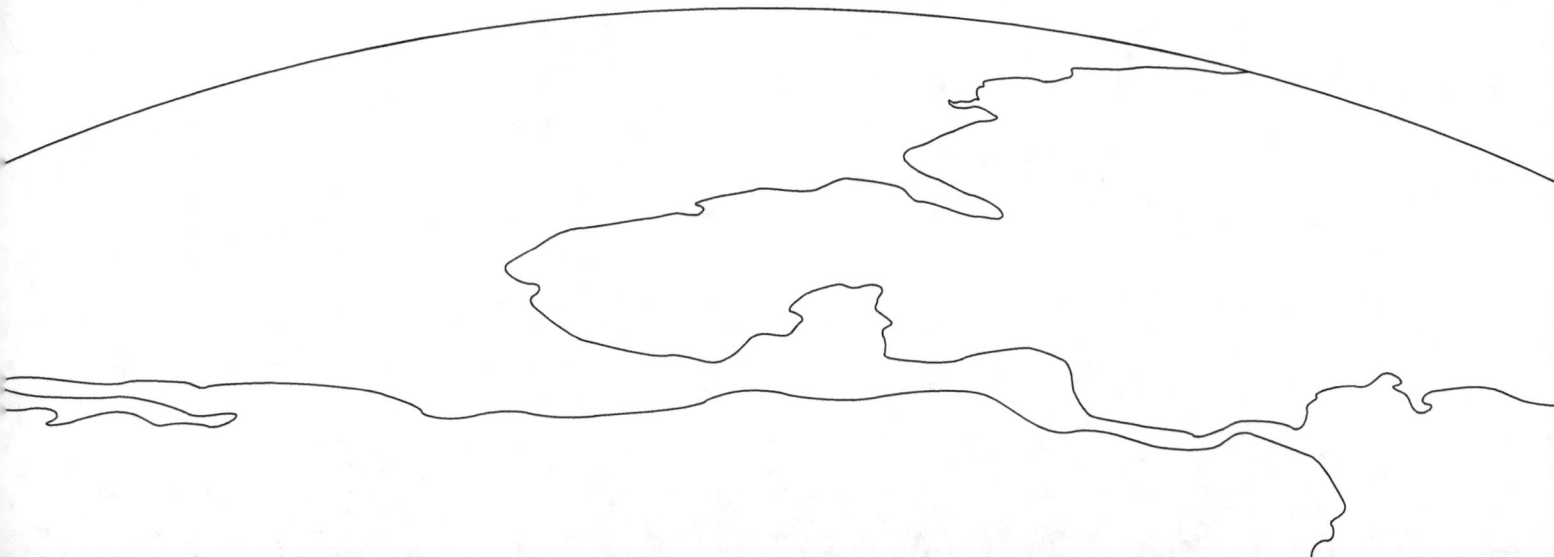

CONTENTS

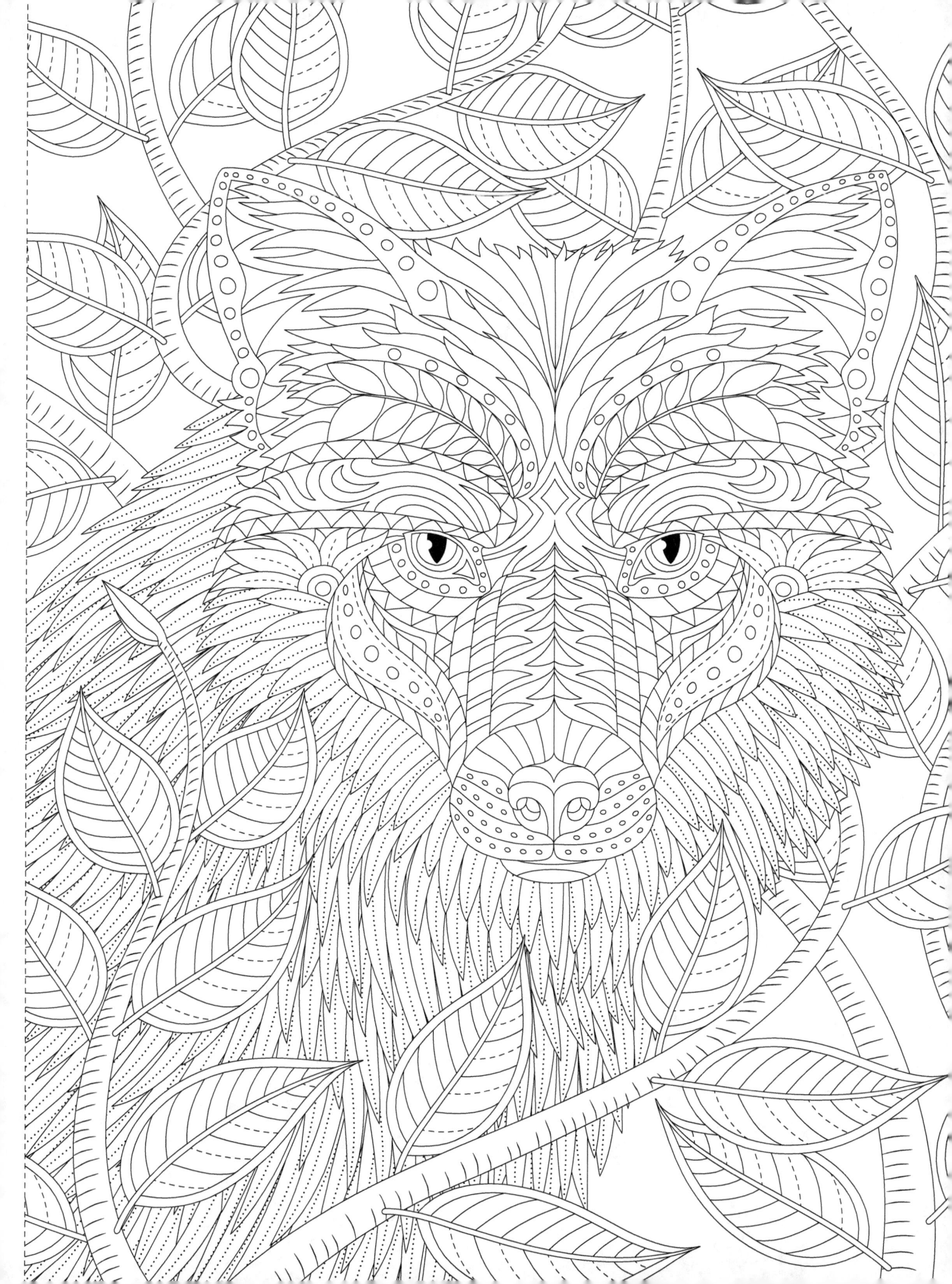

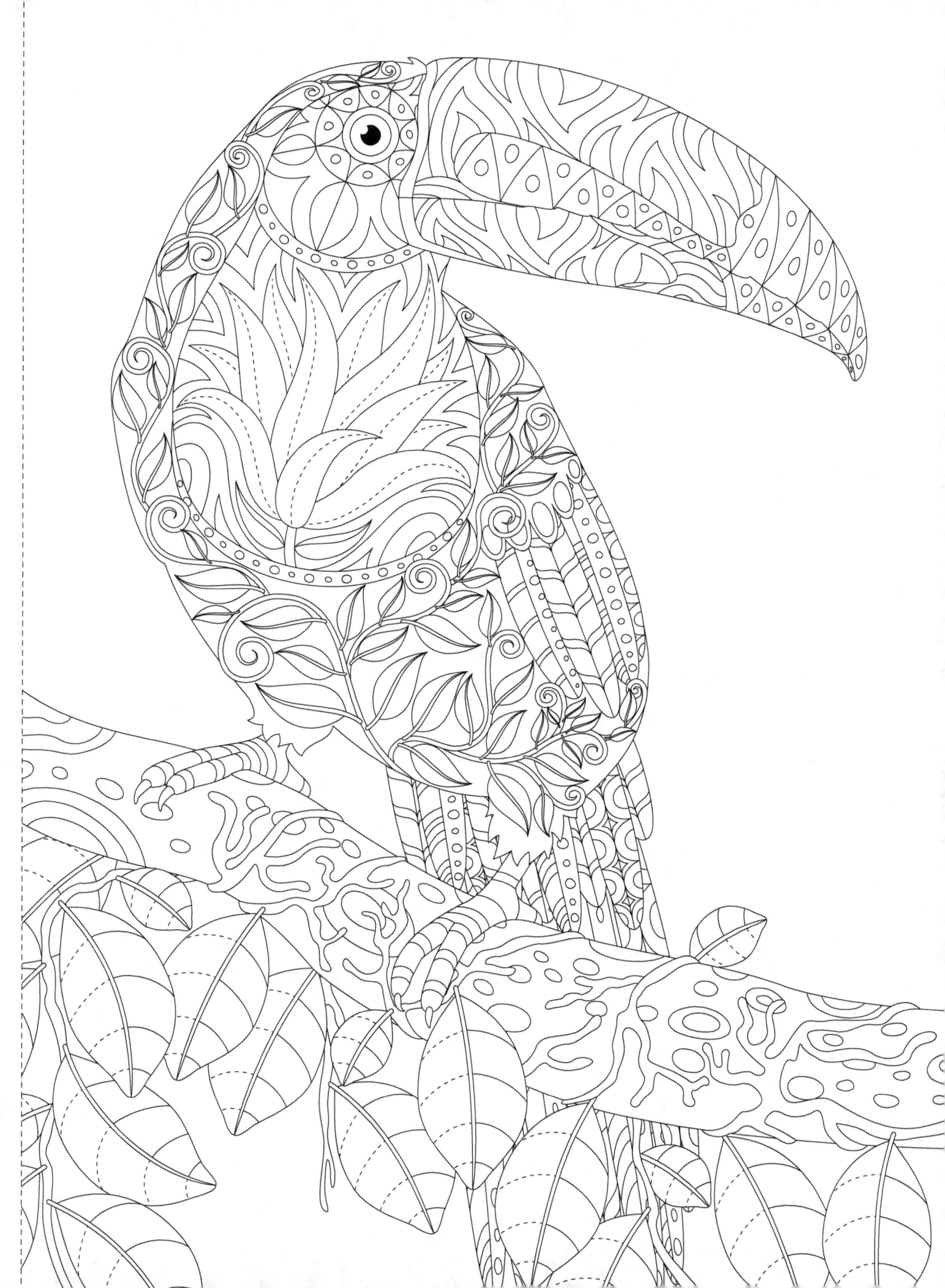

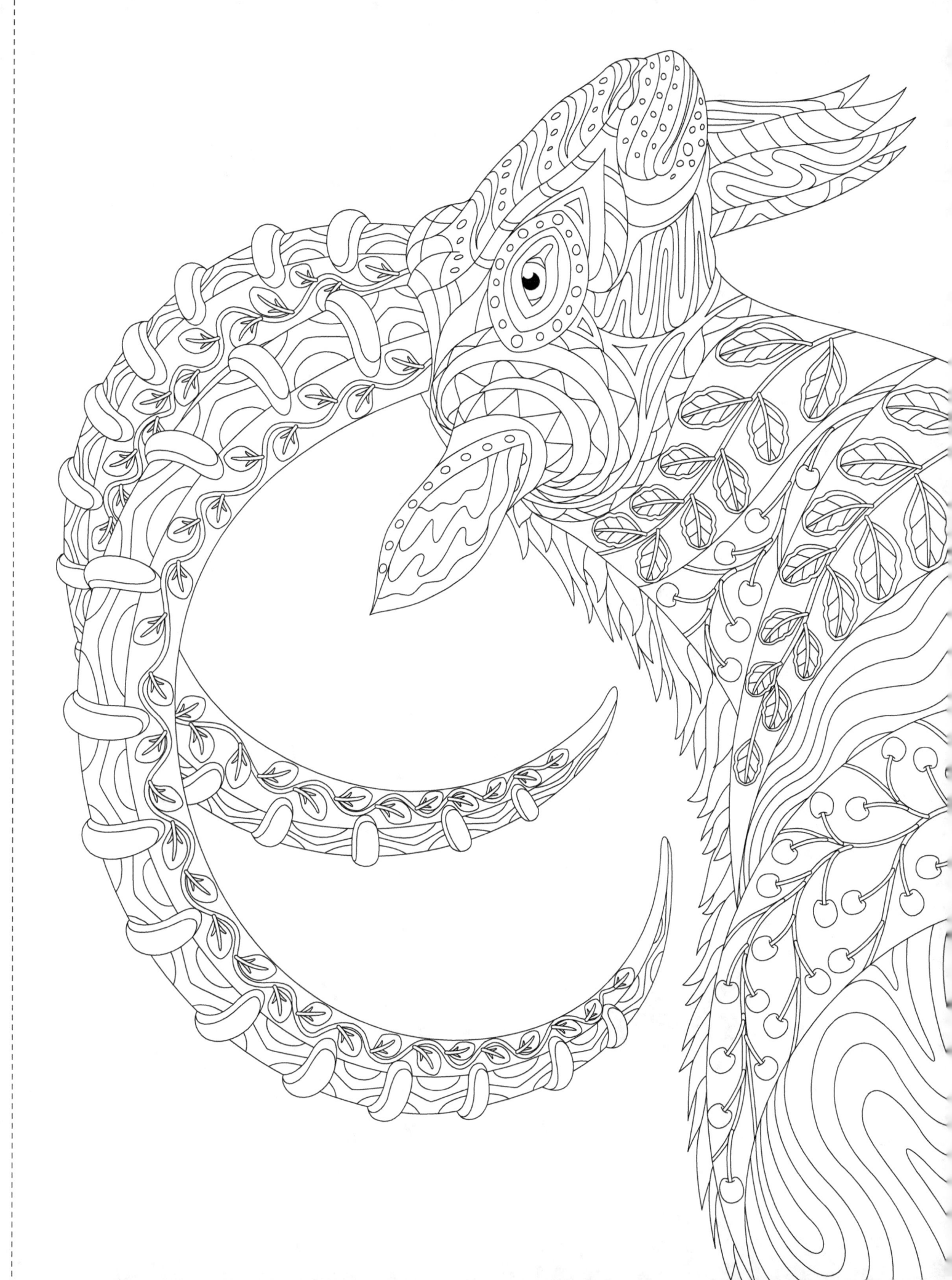

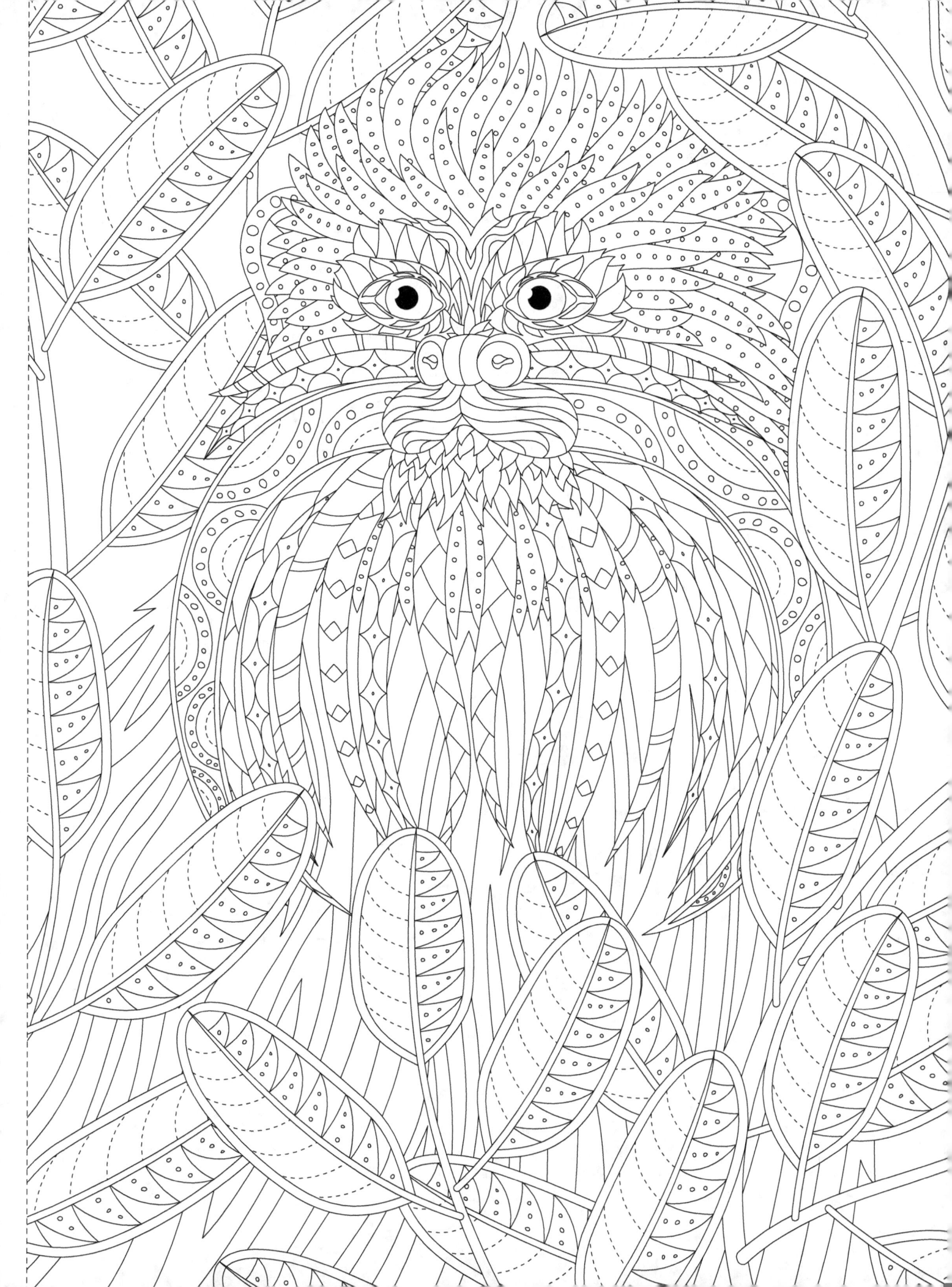

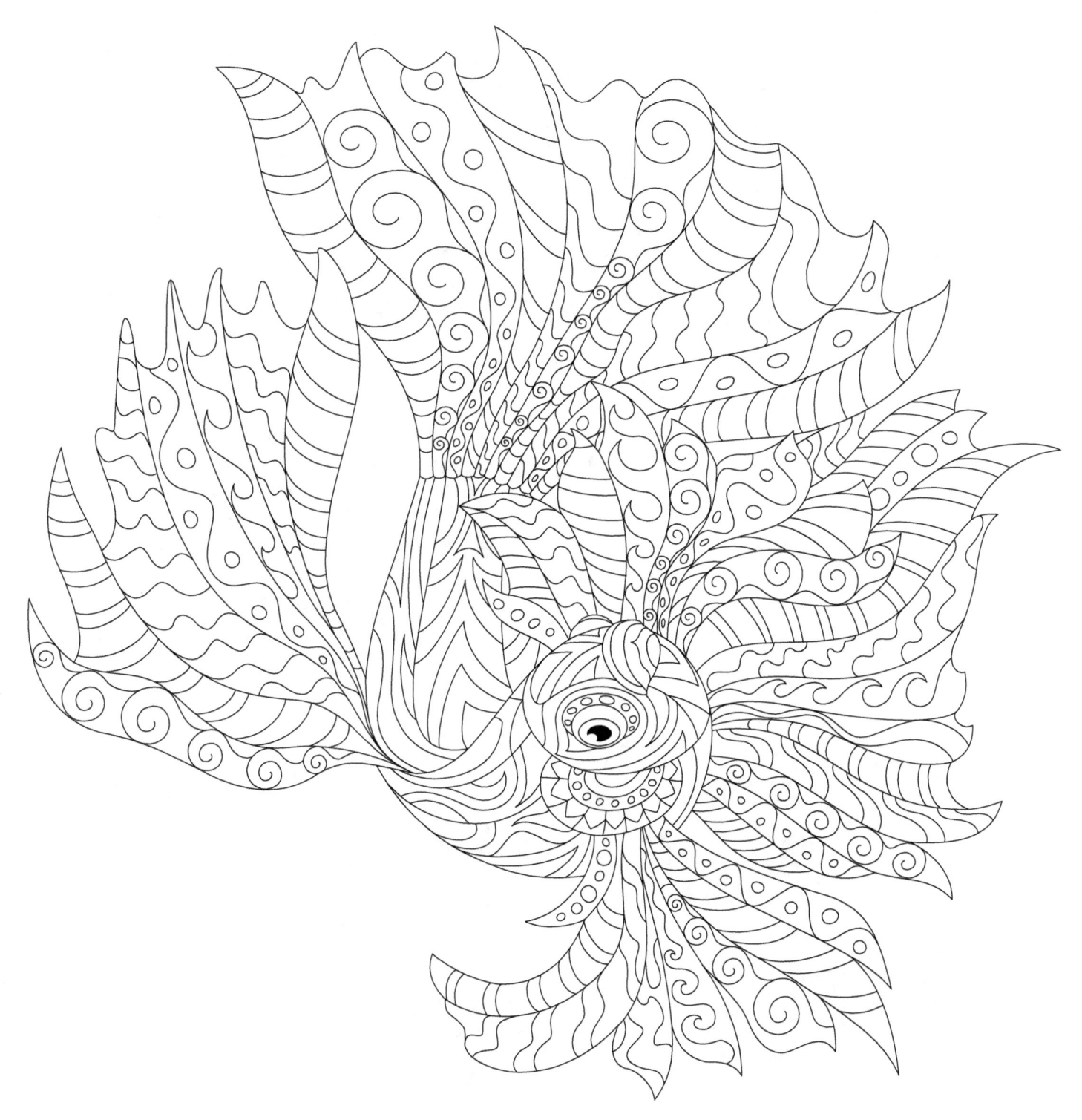

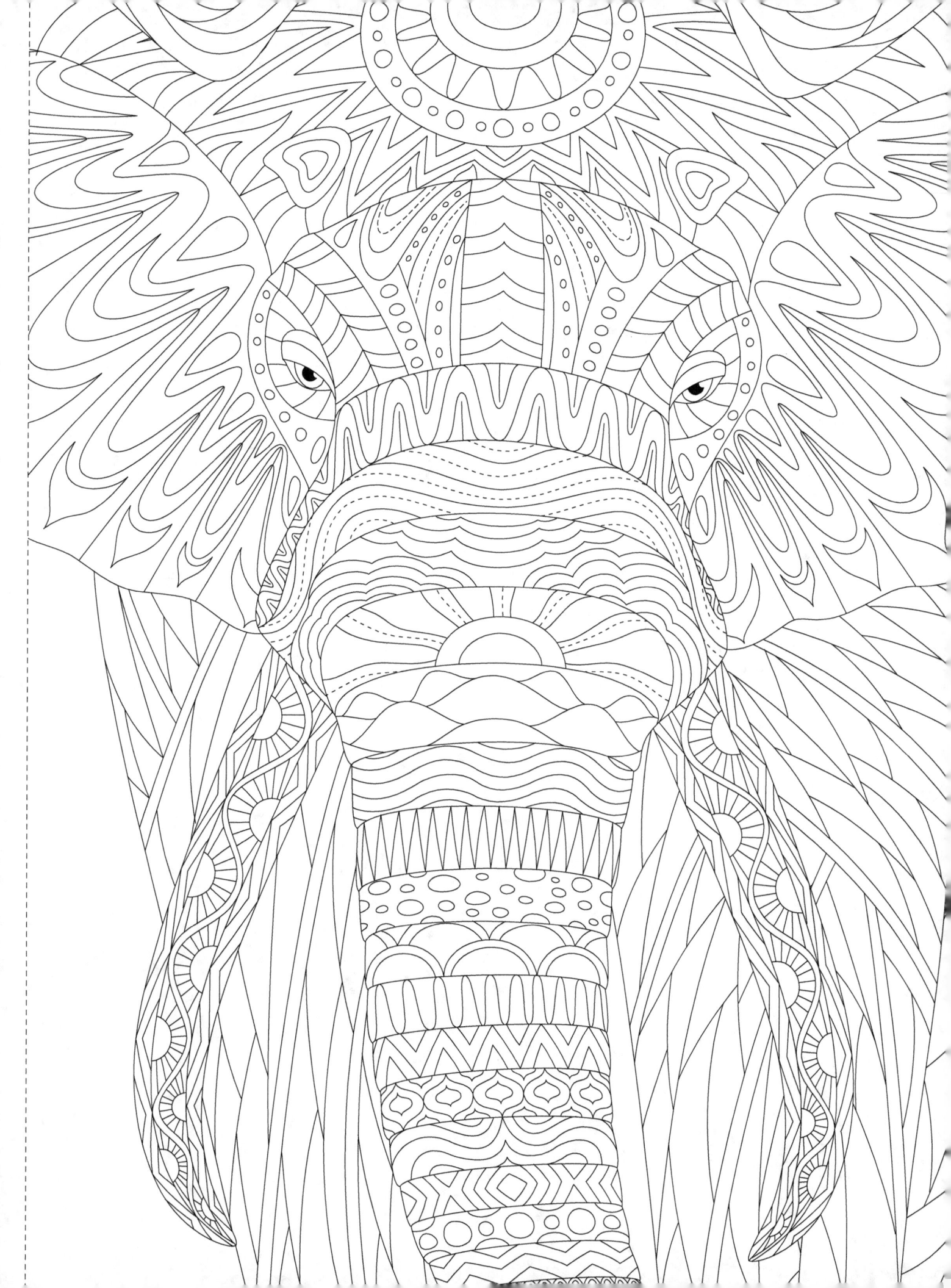

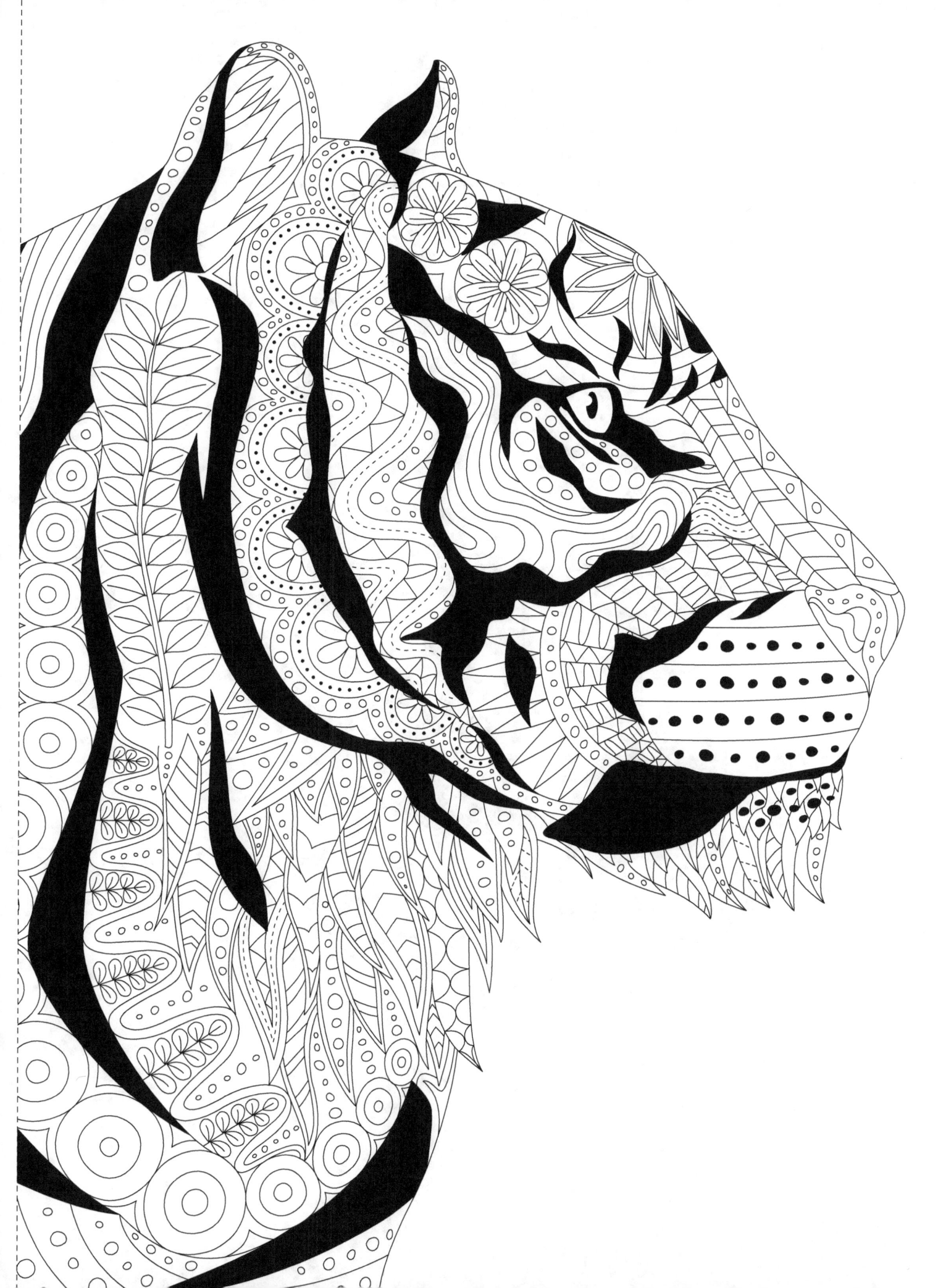

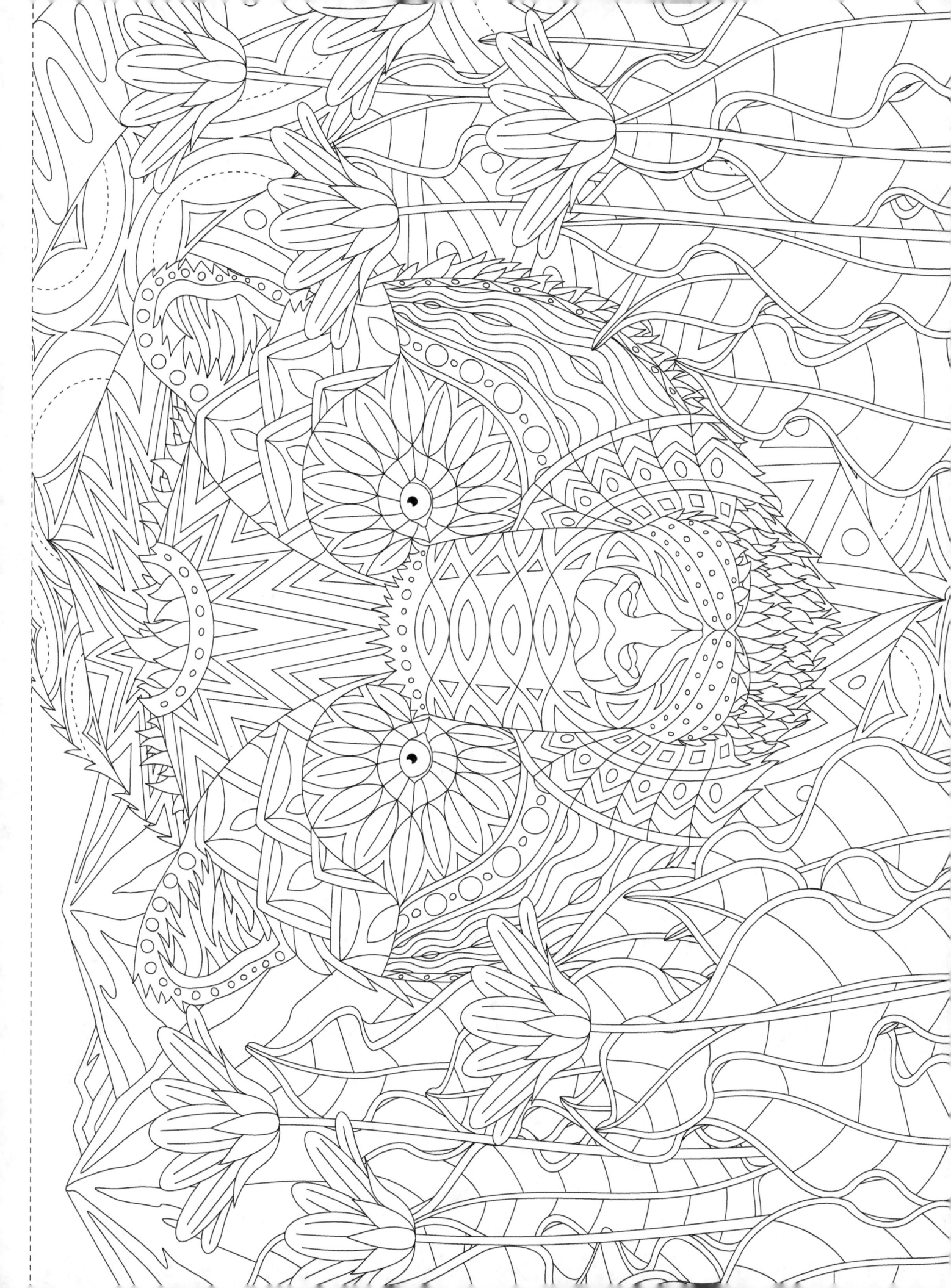

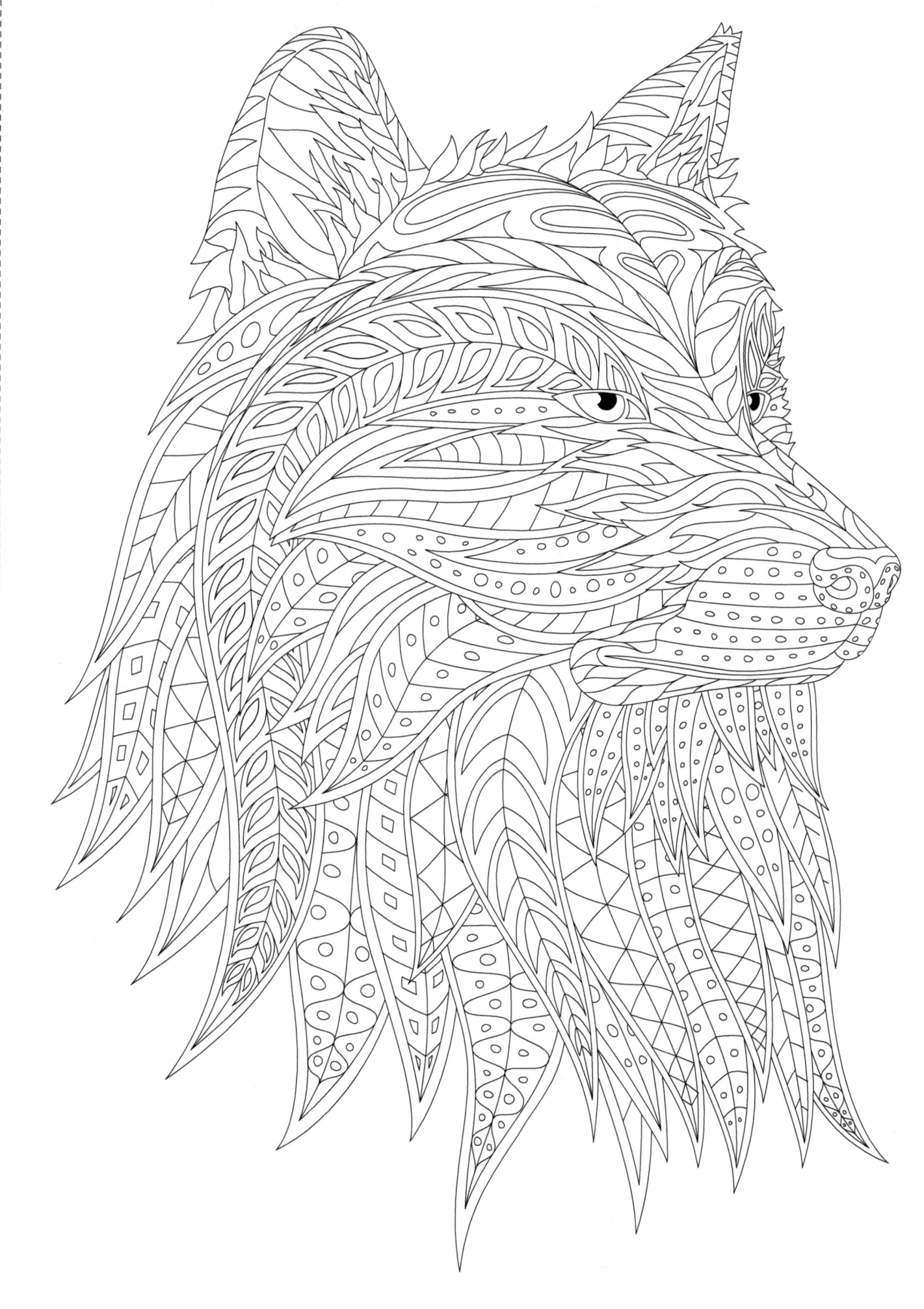

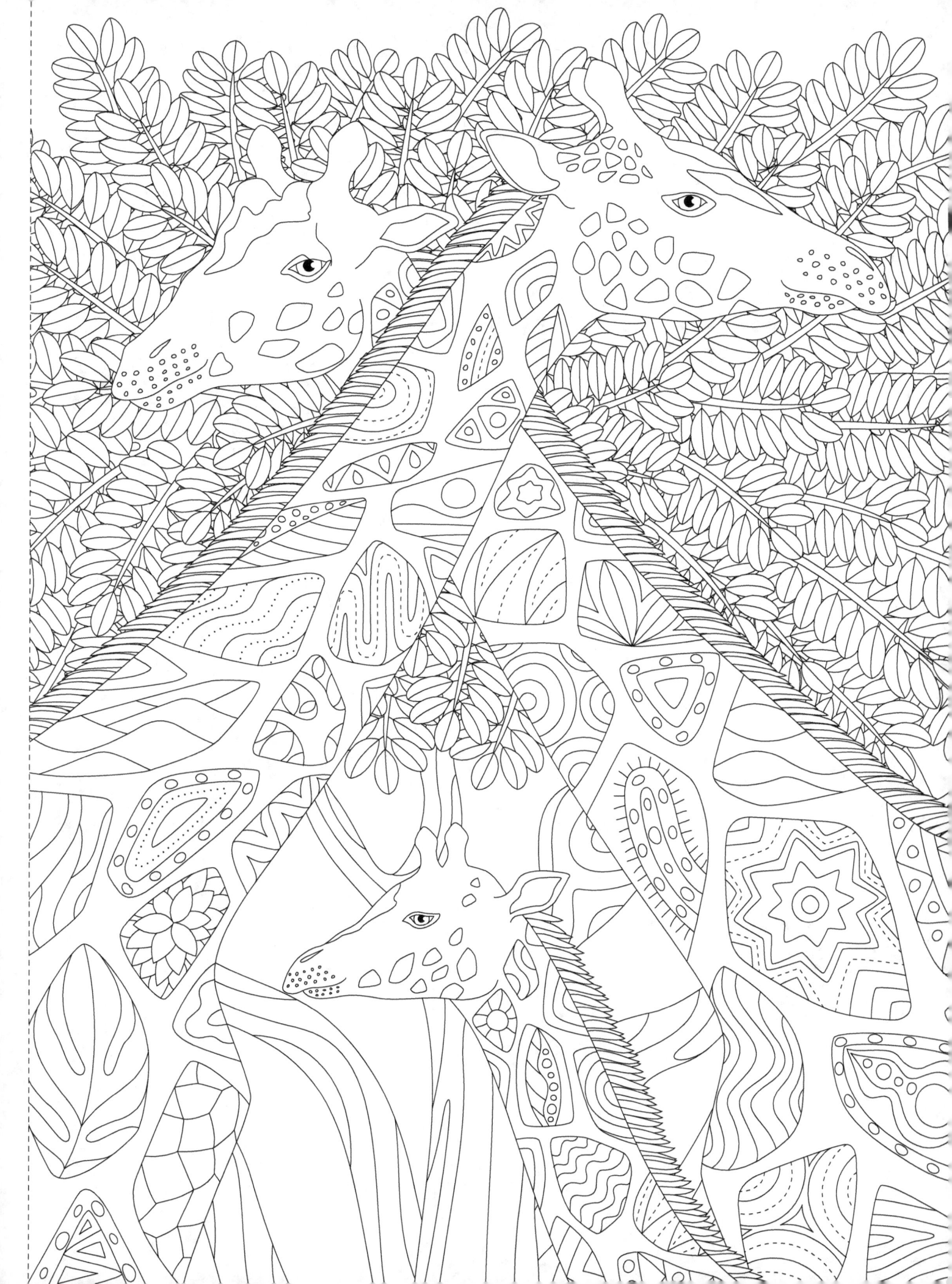

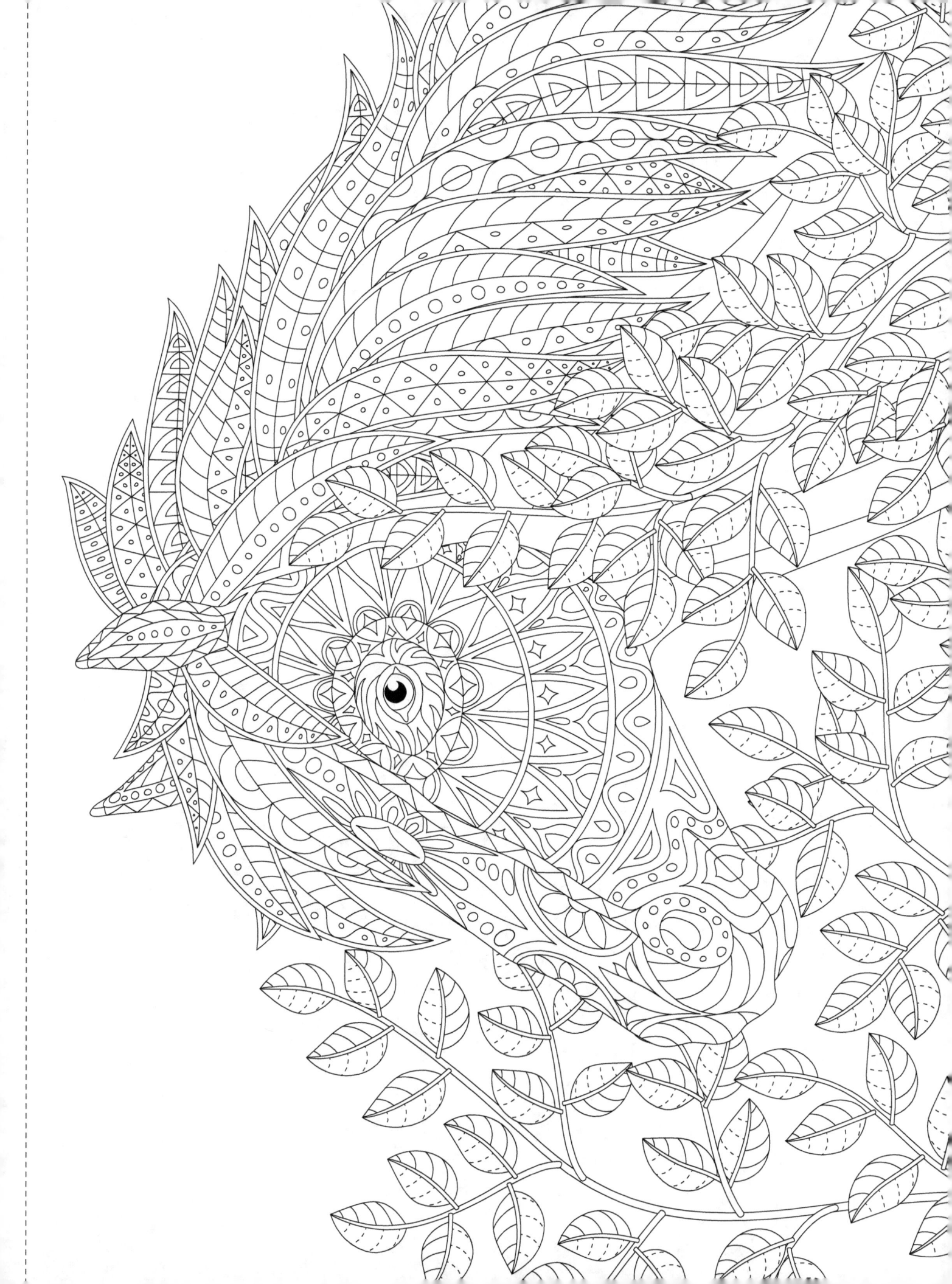

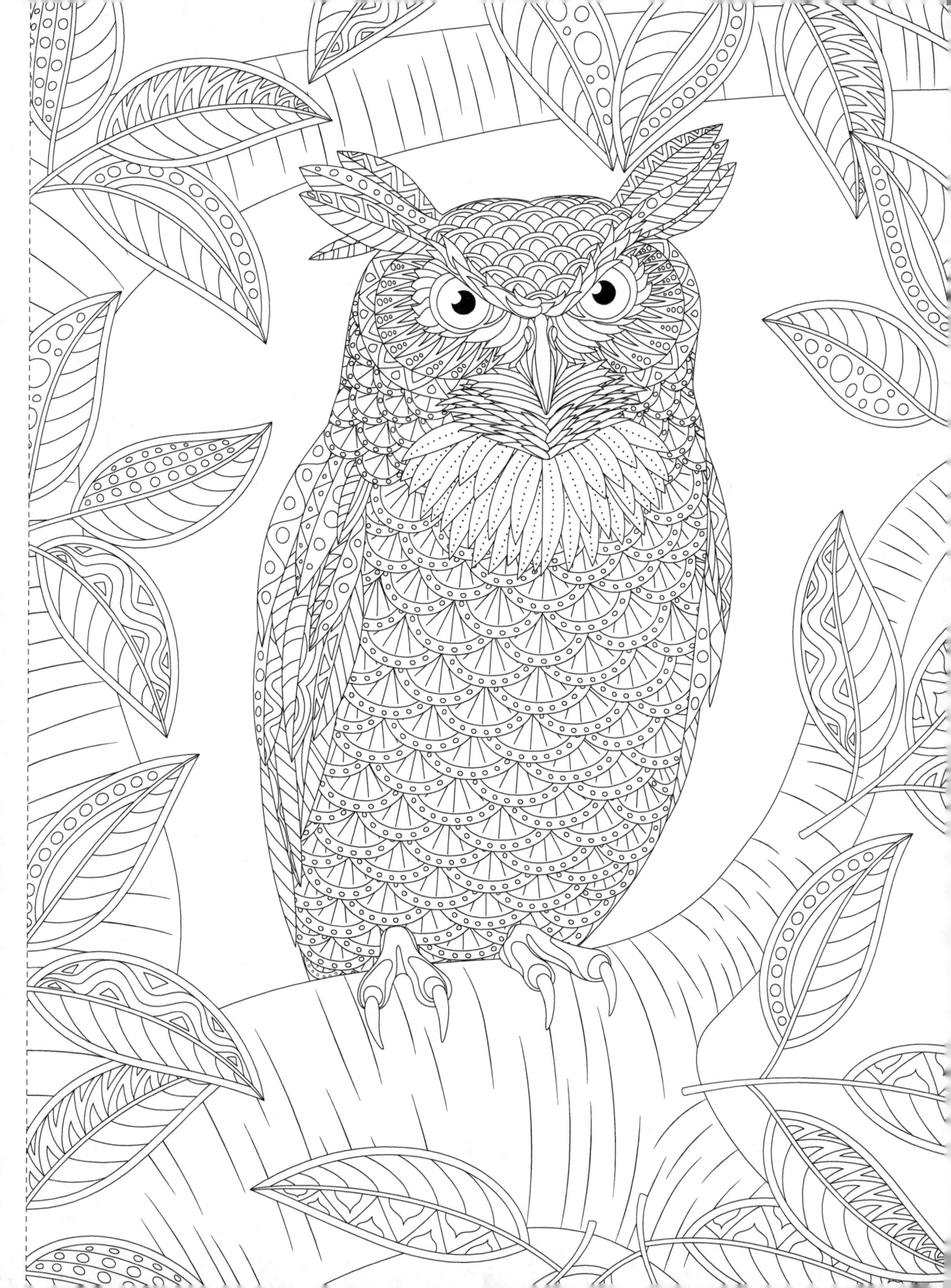

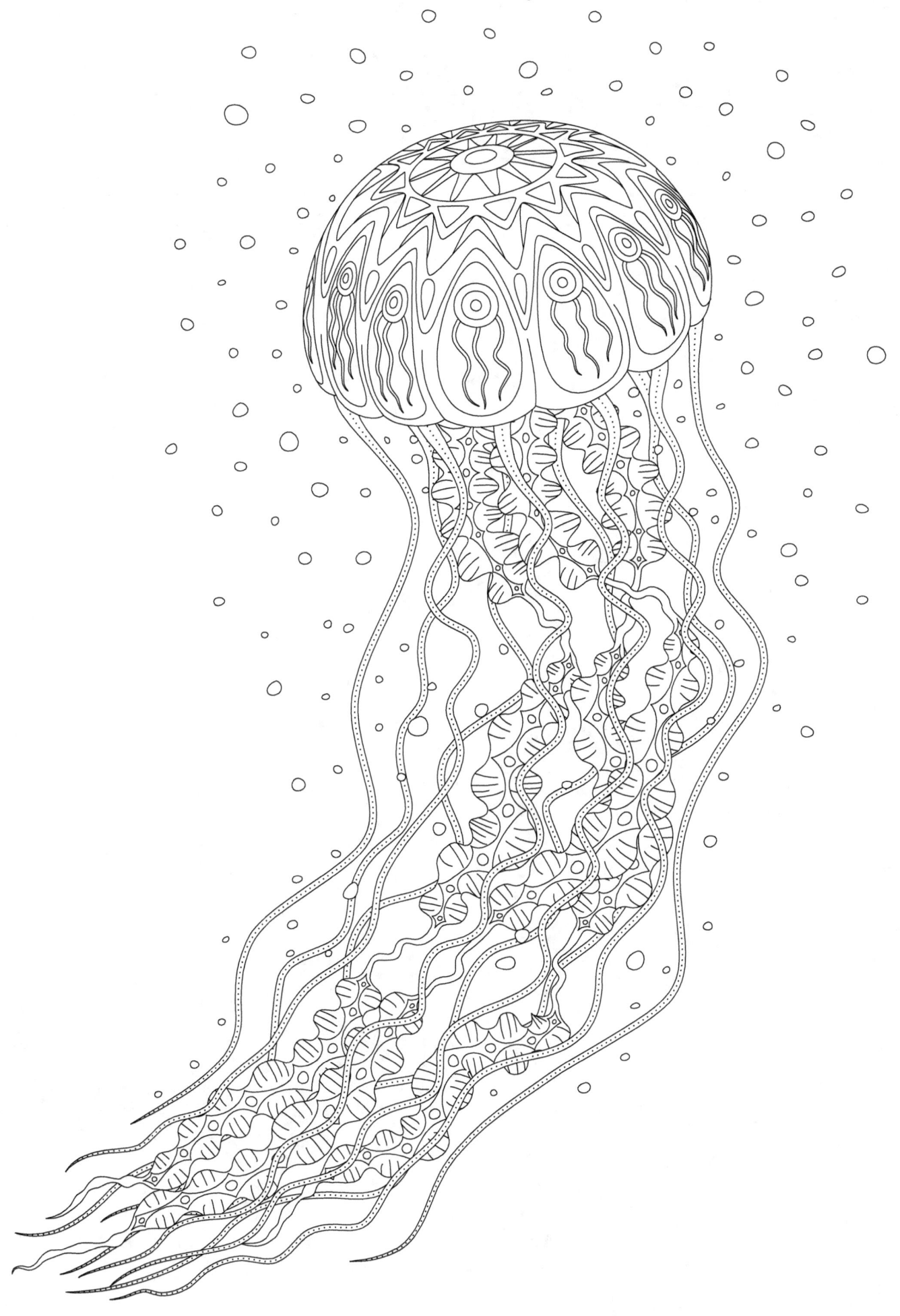

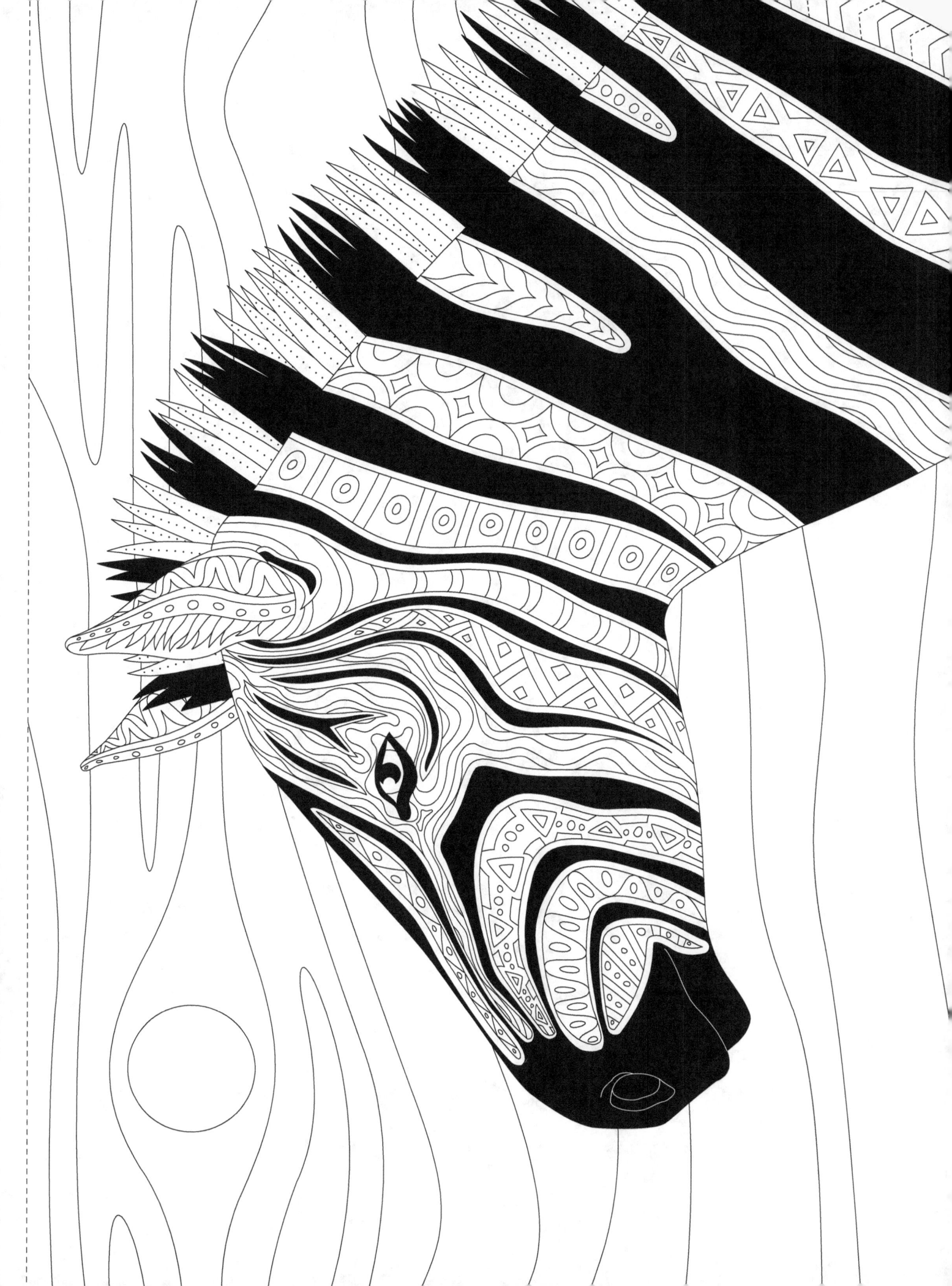

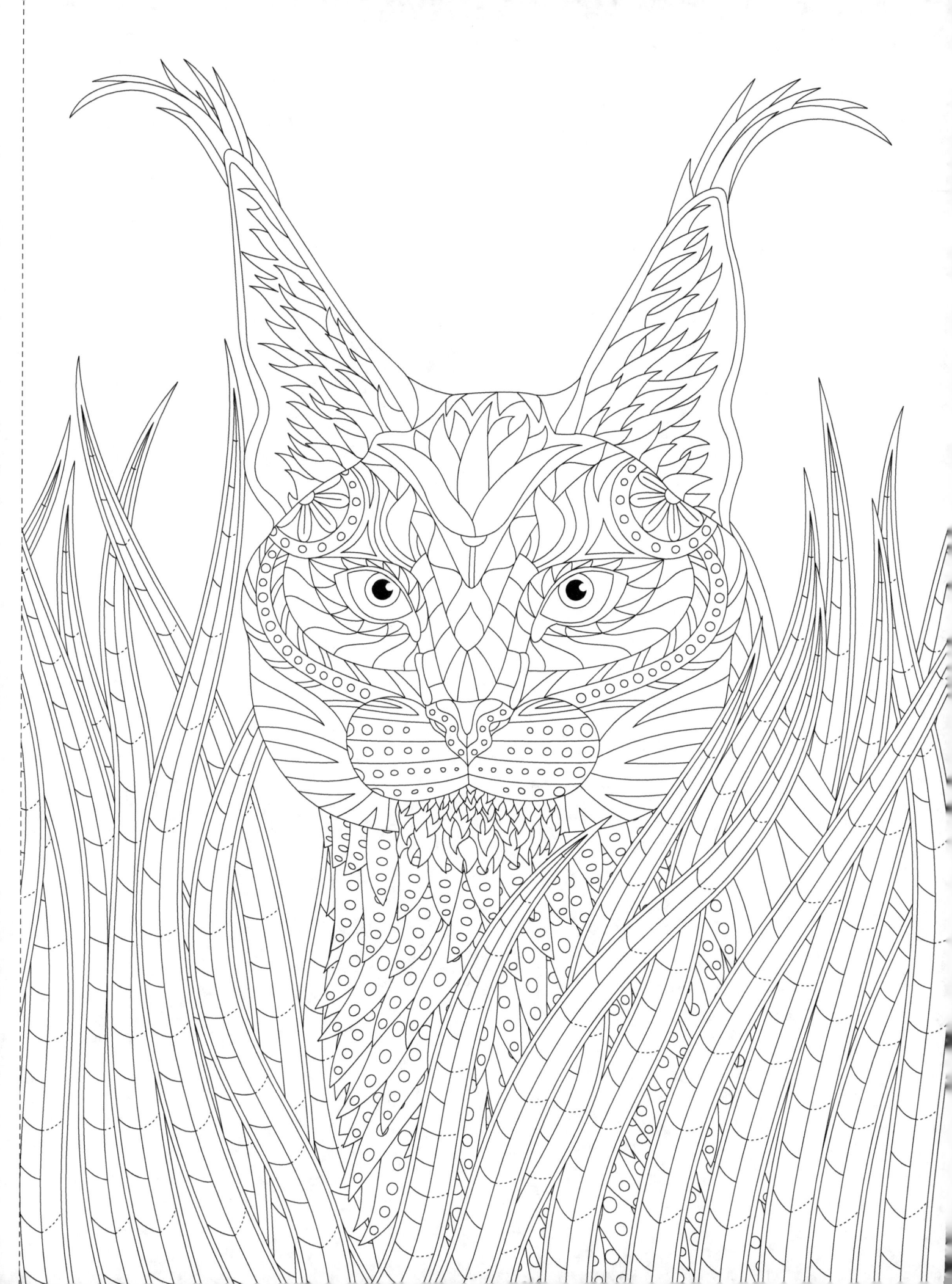

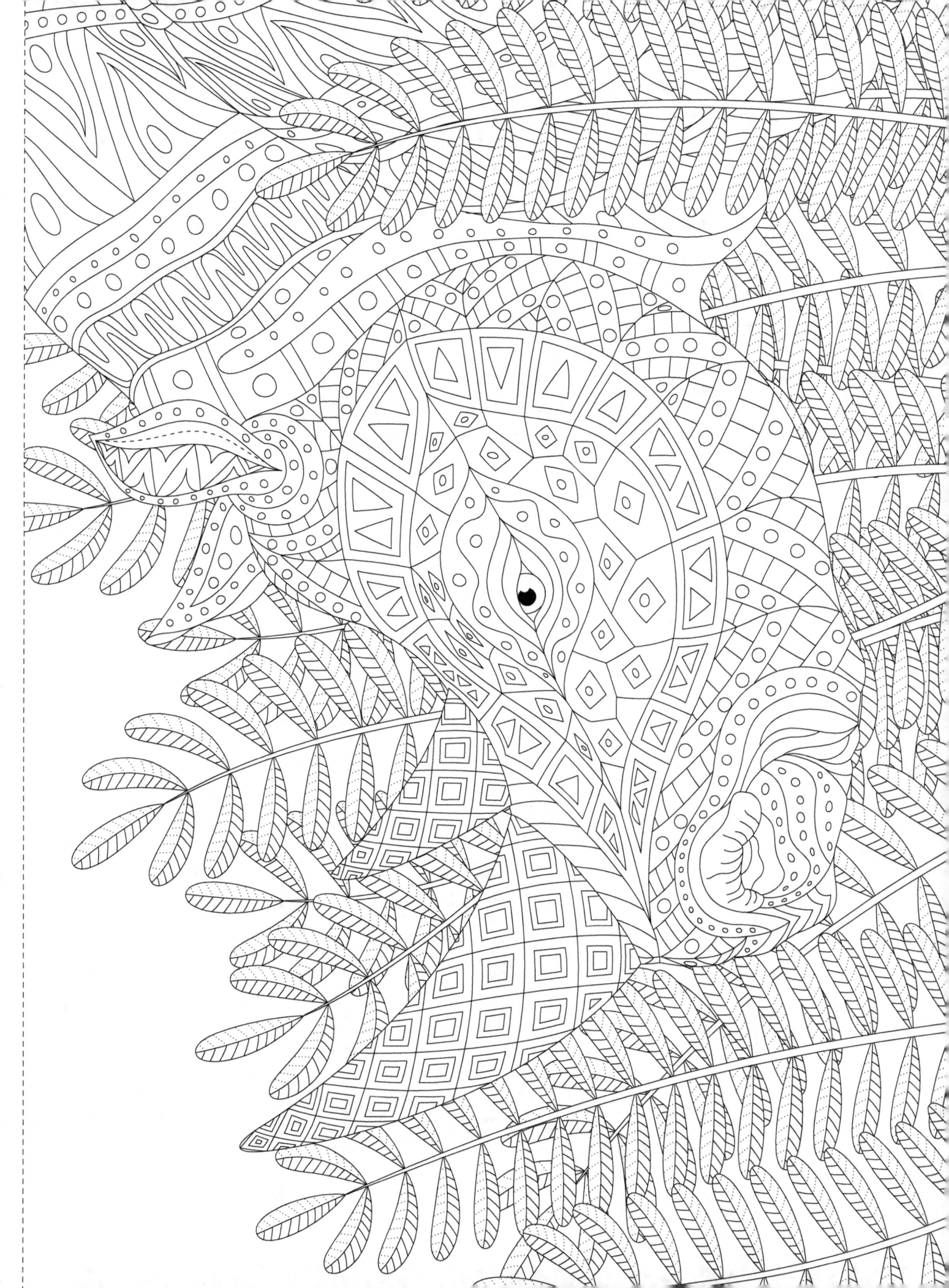

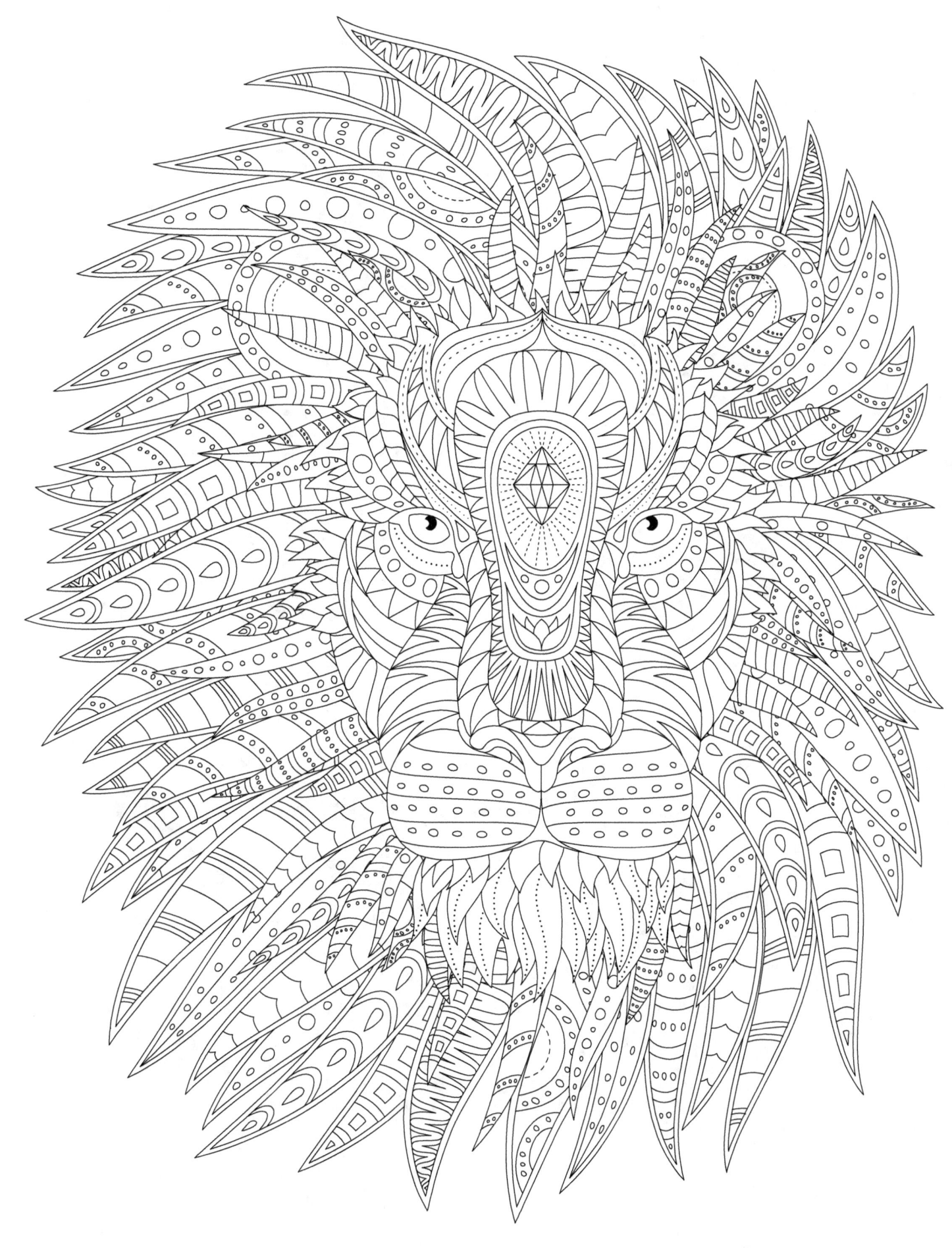

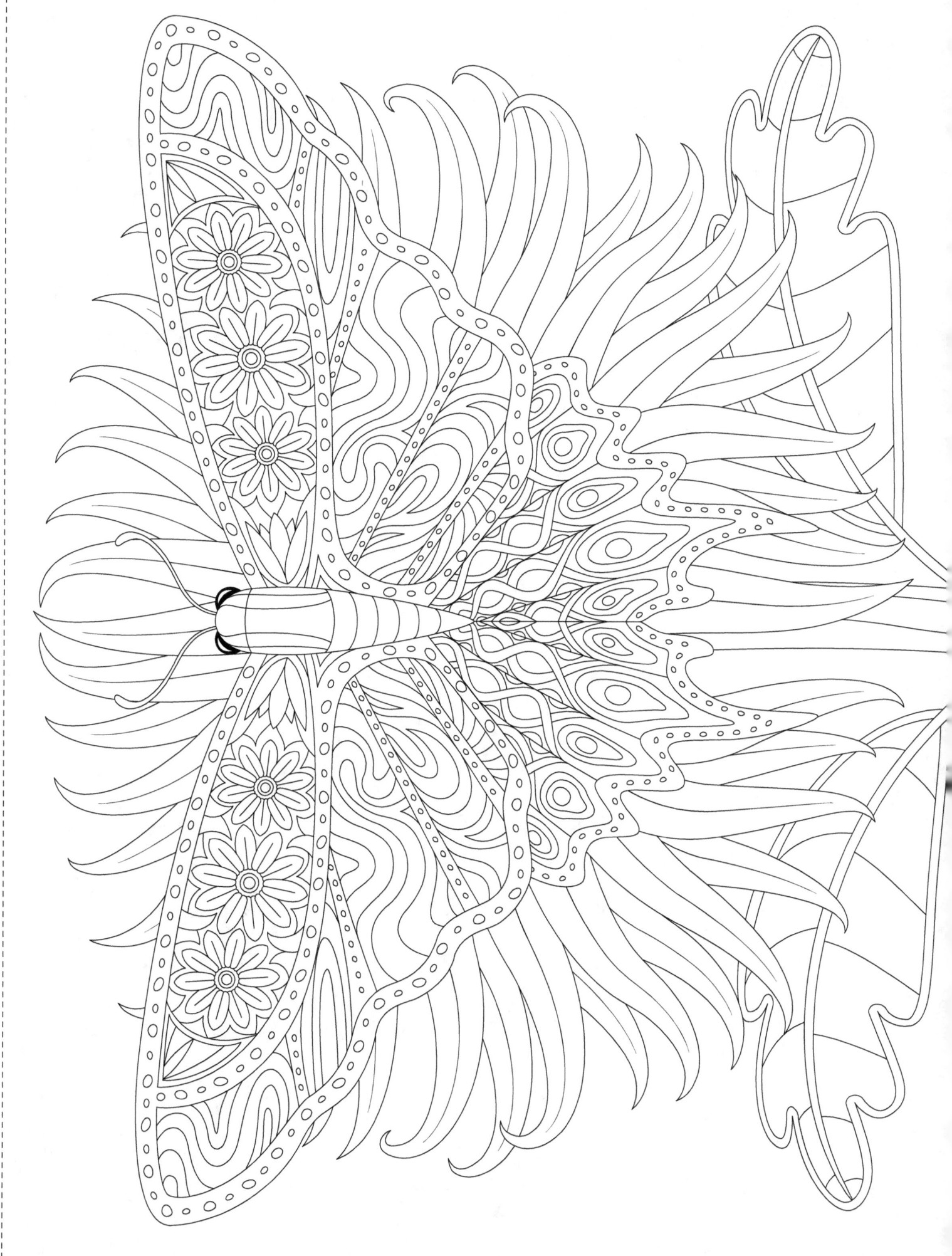

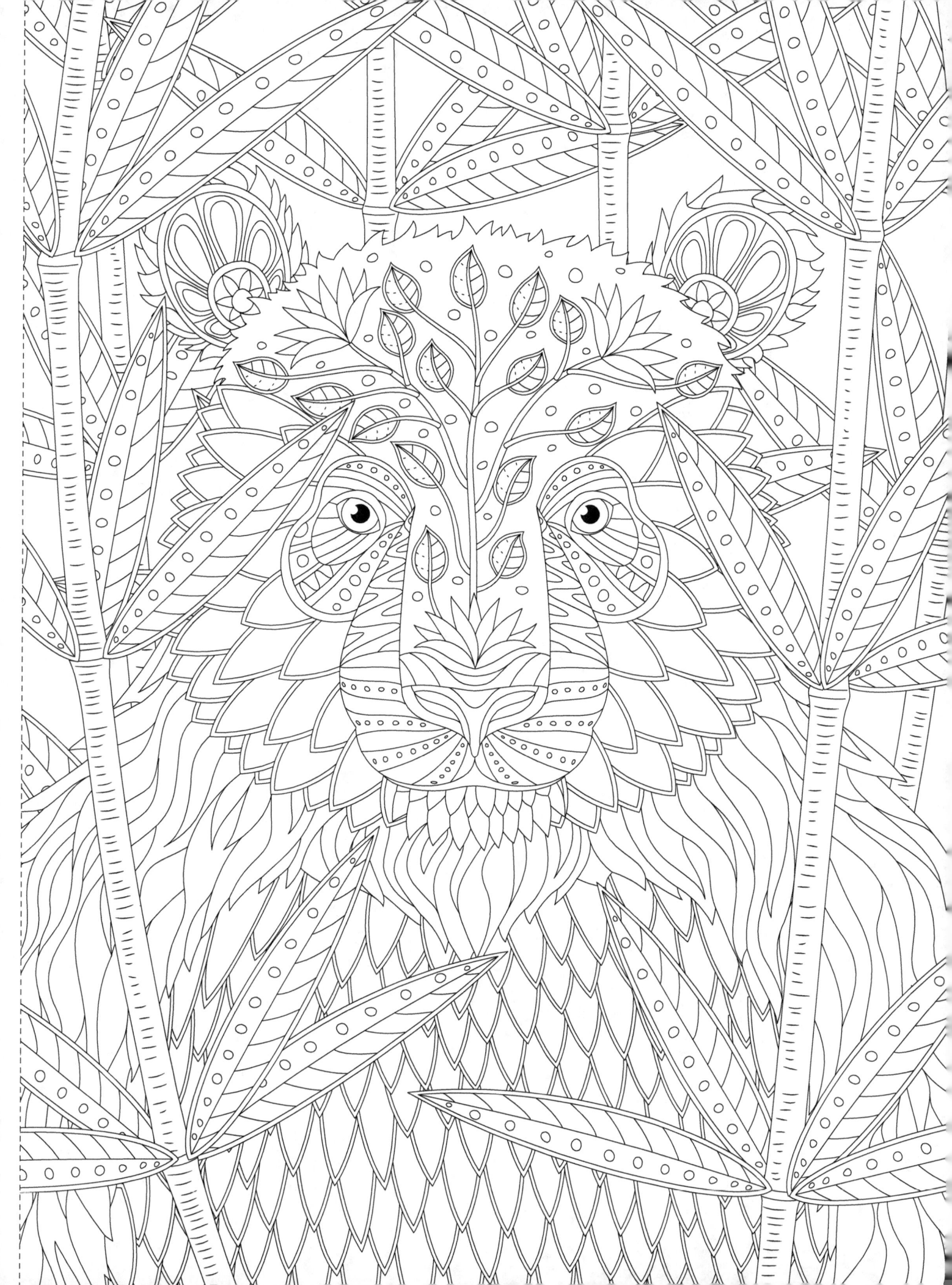

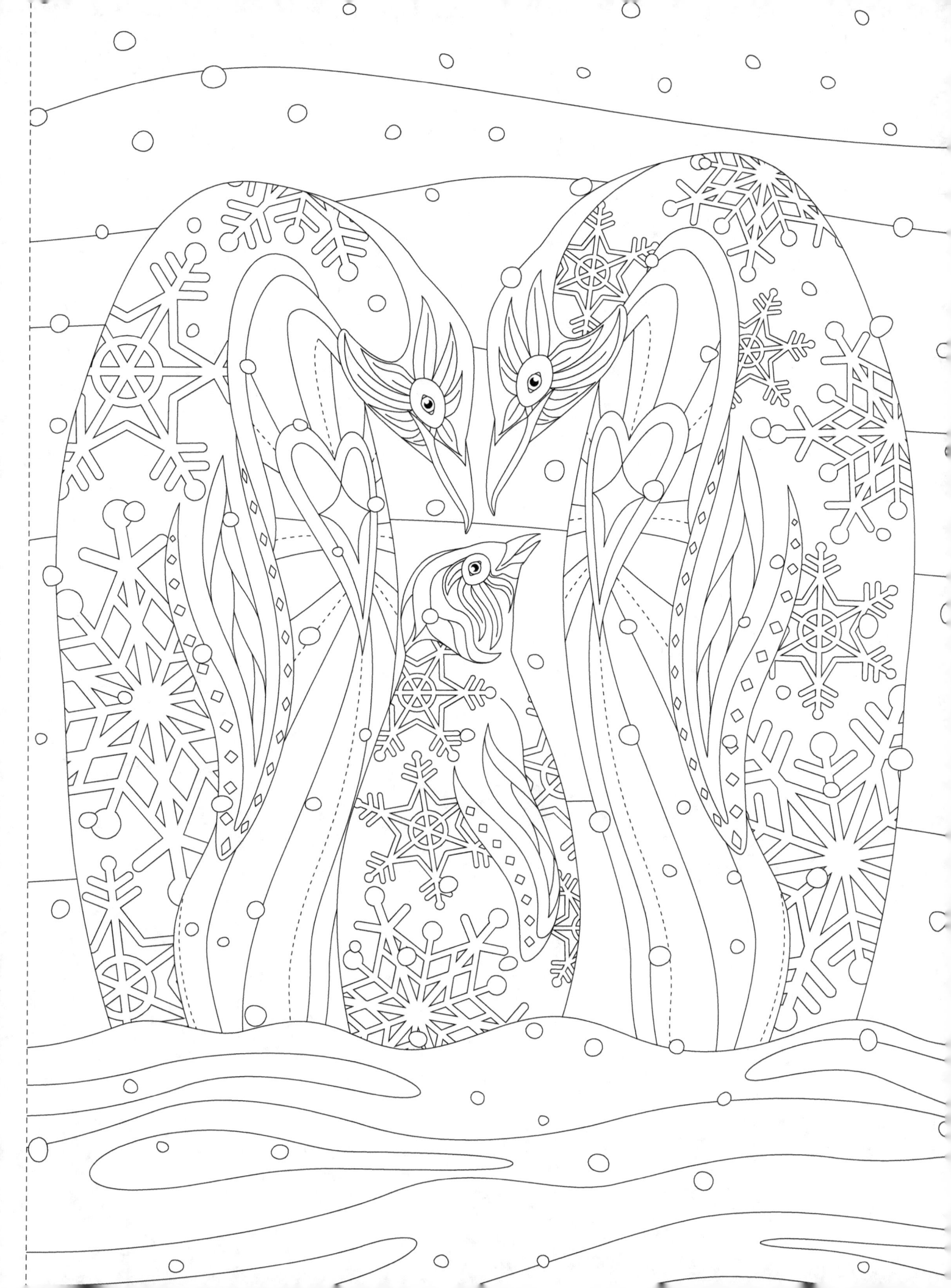

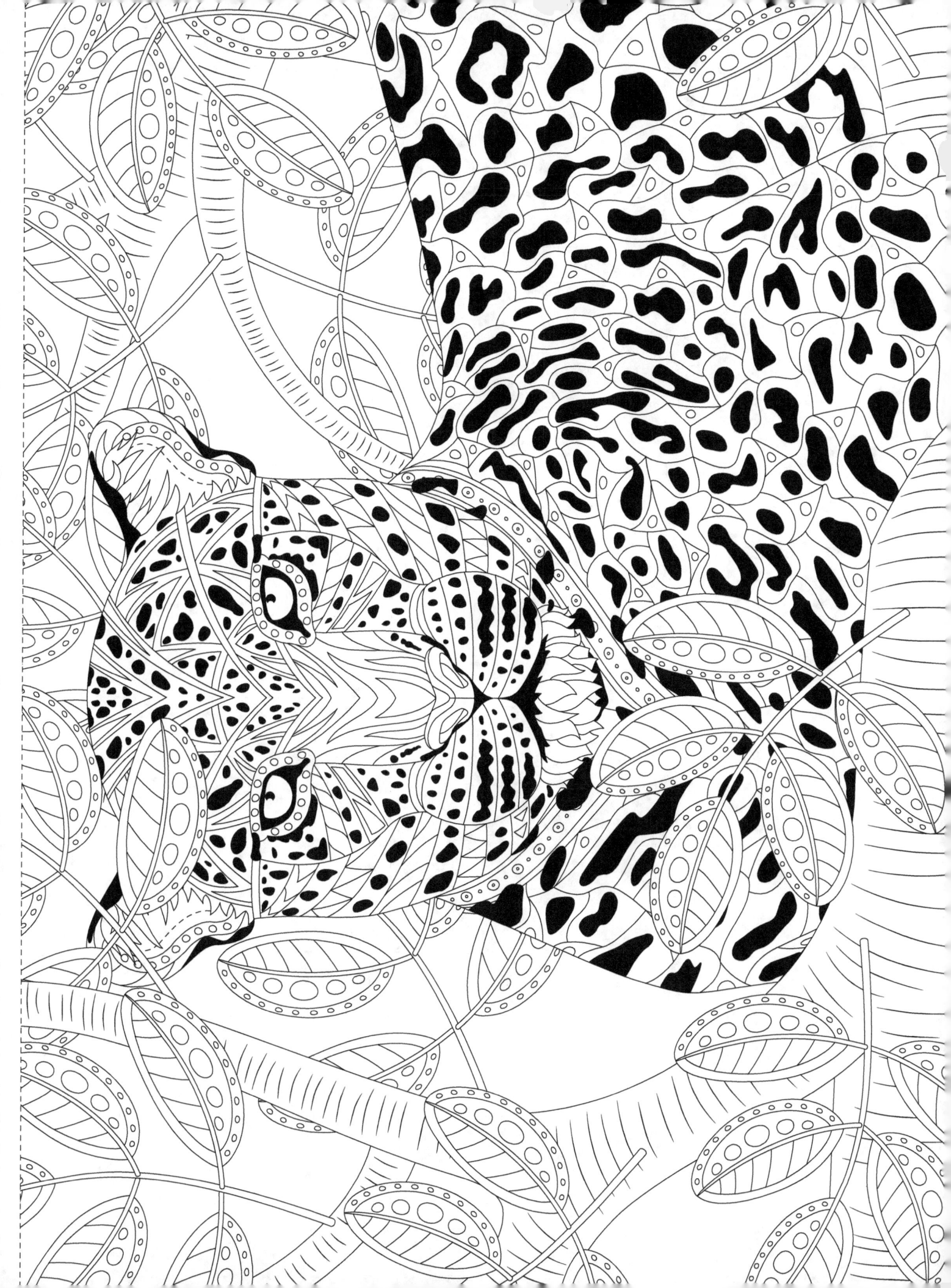

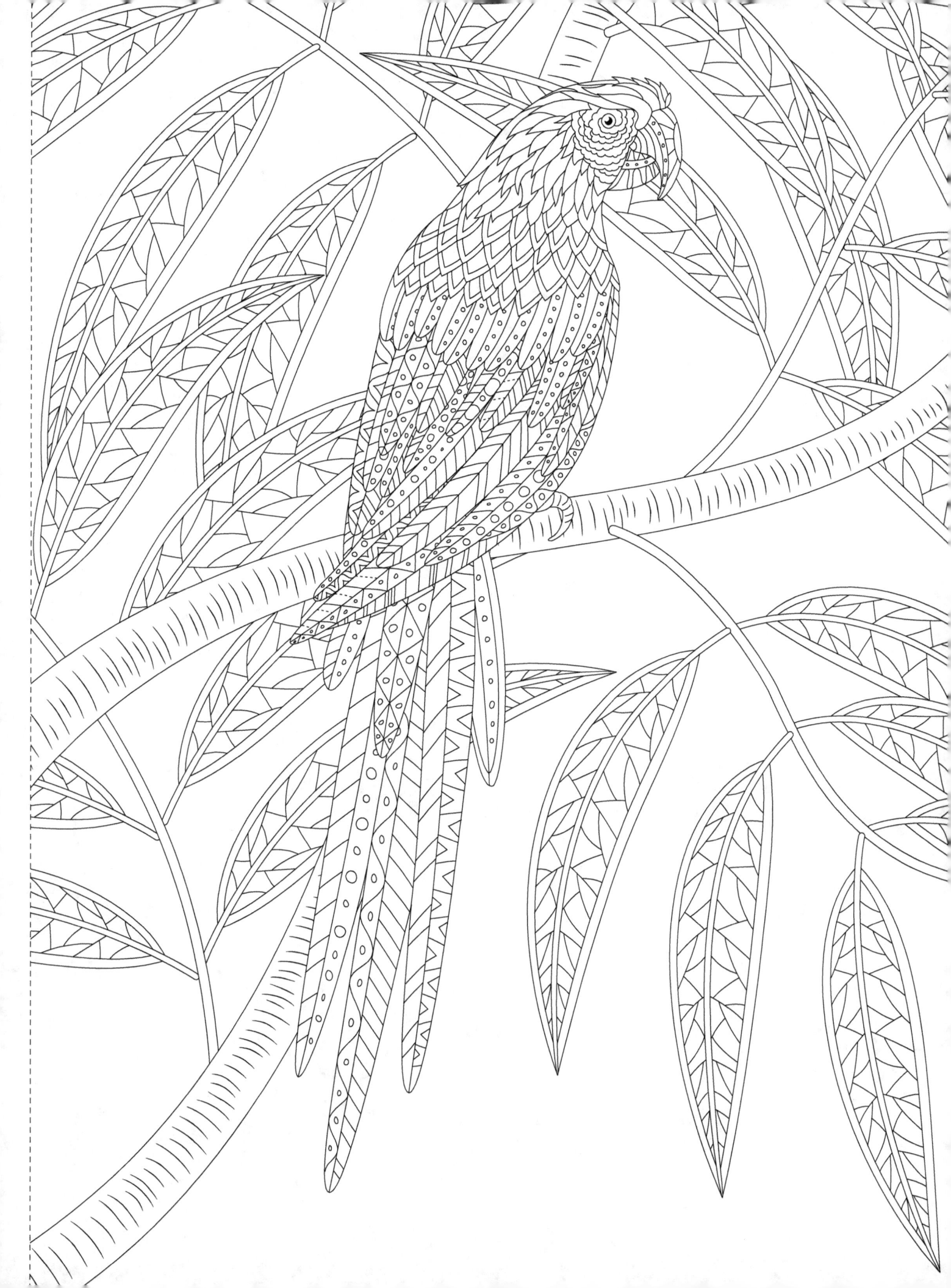

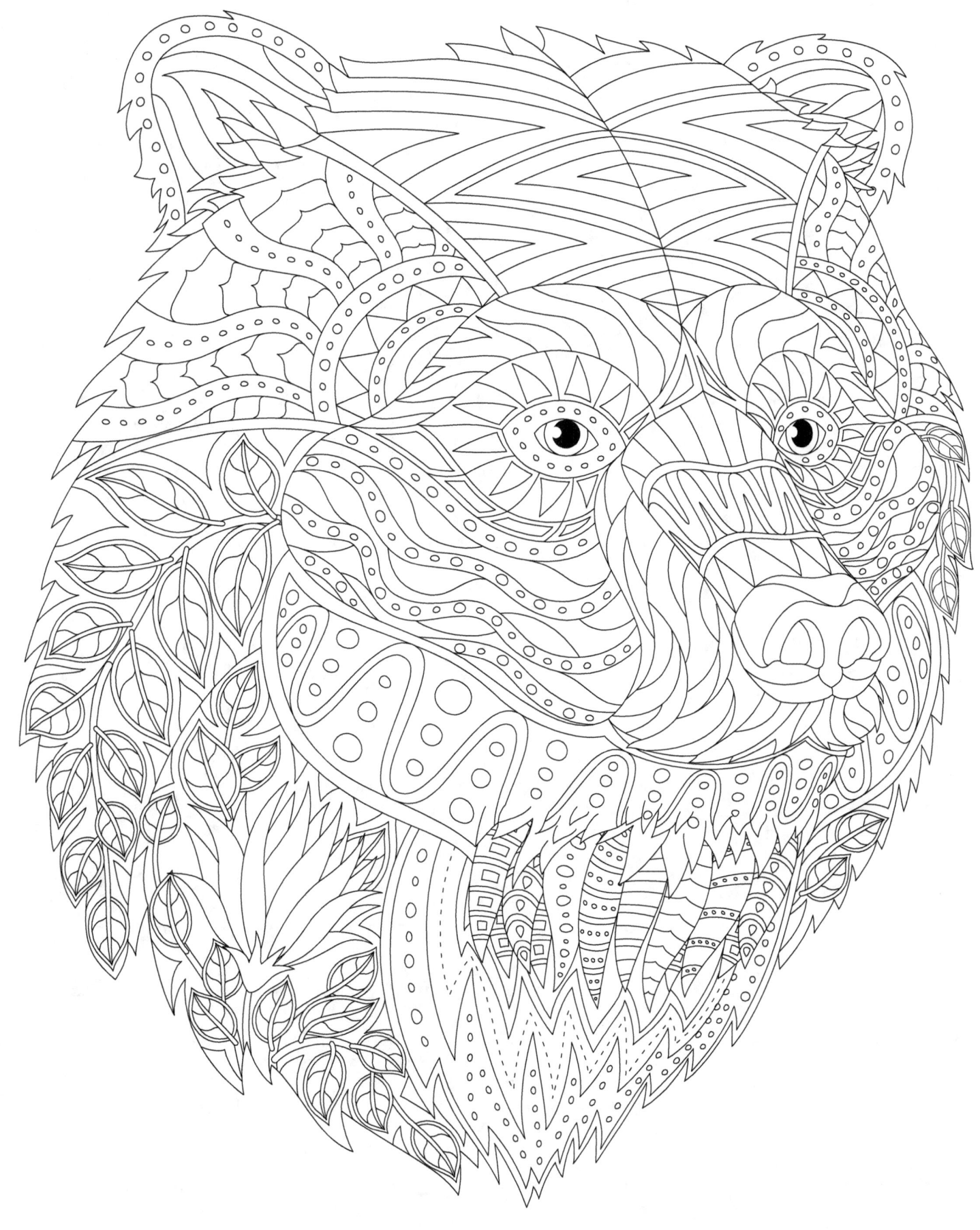

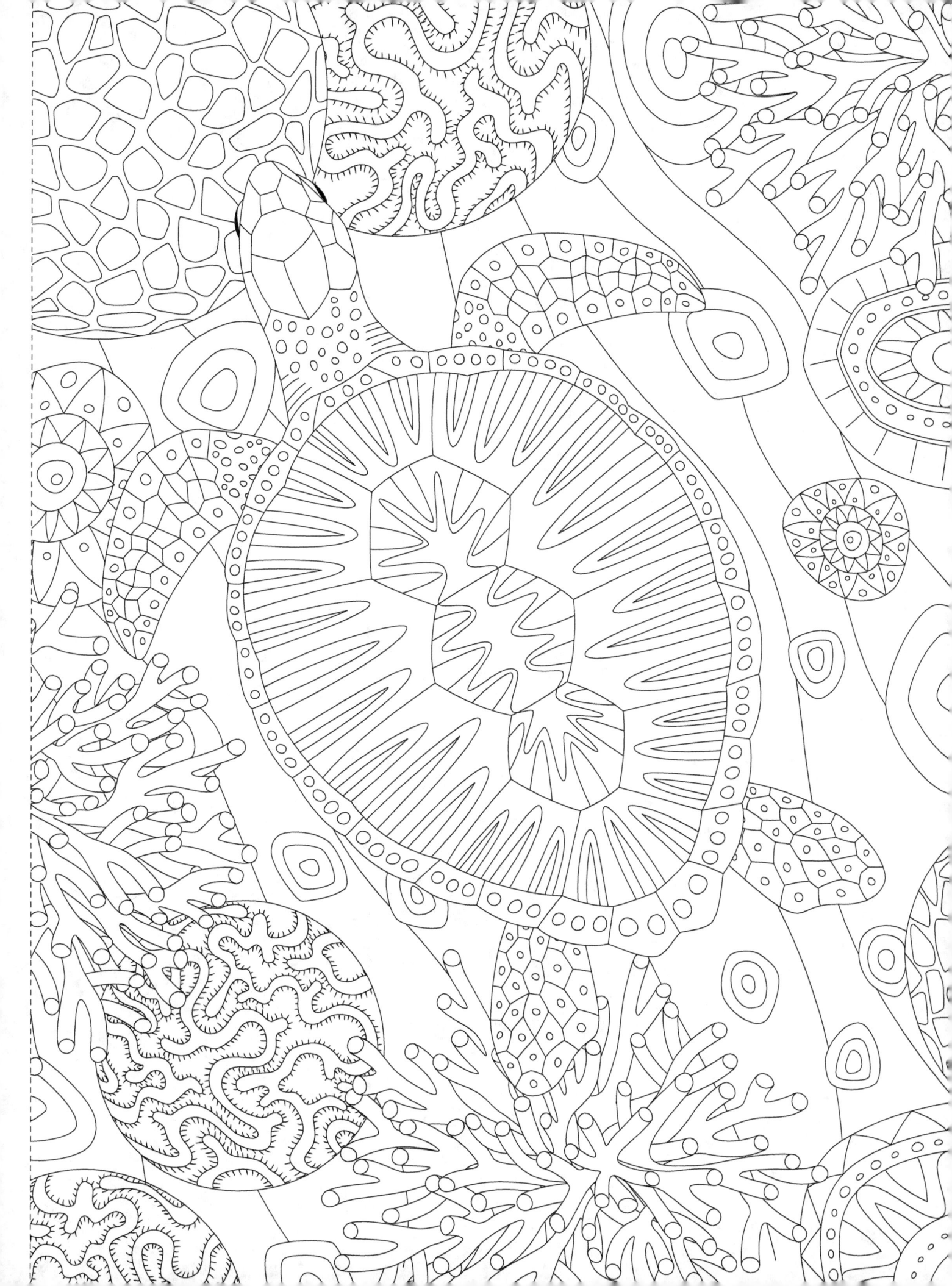

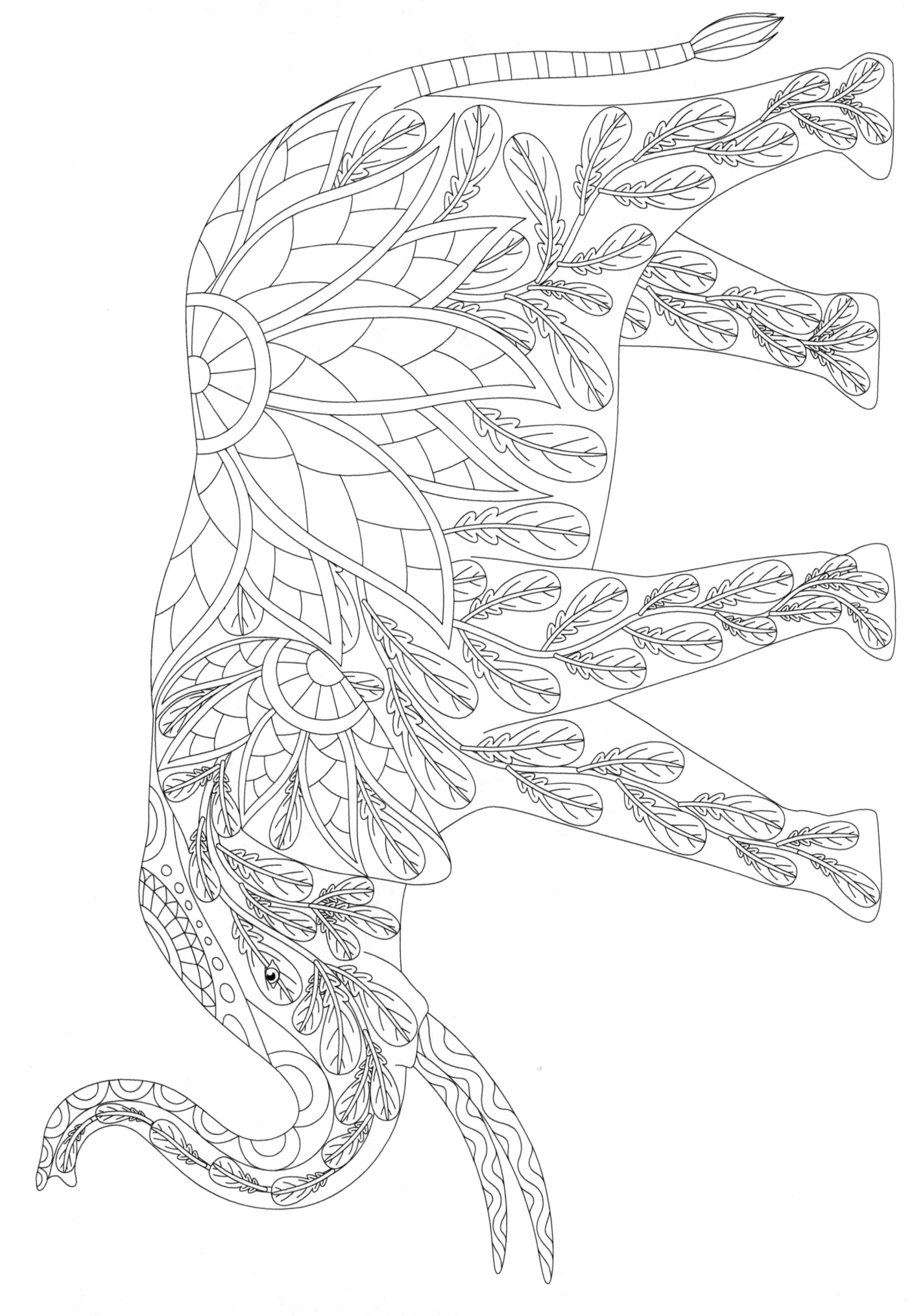

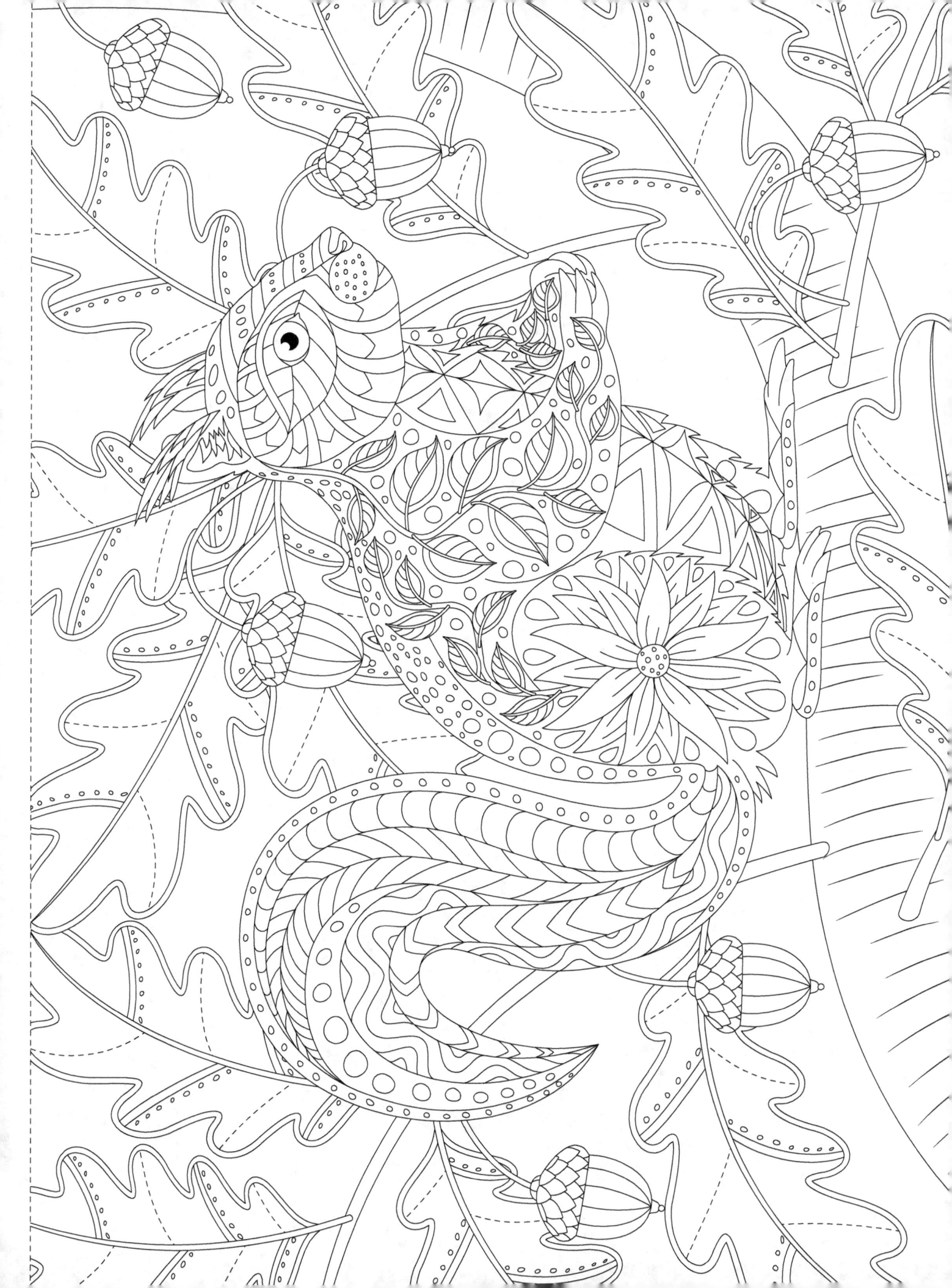

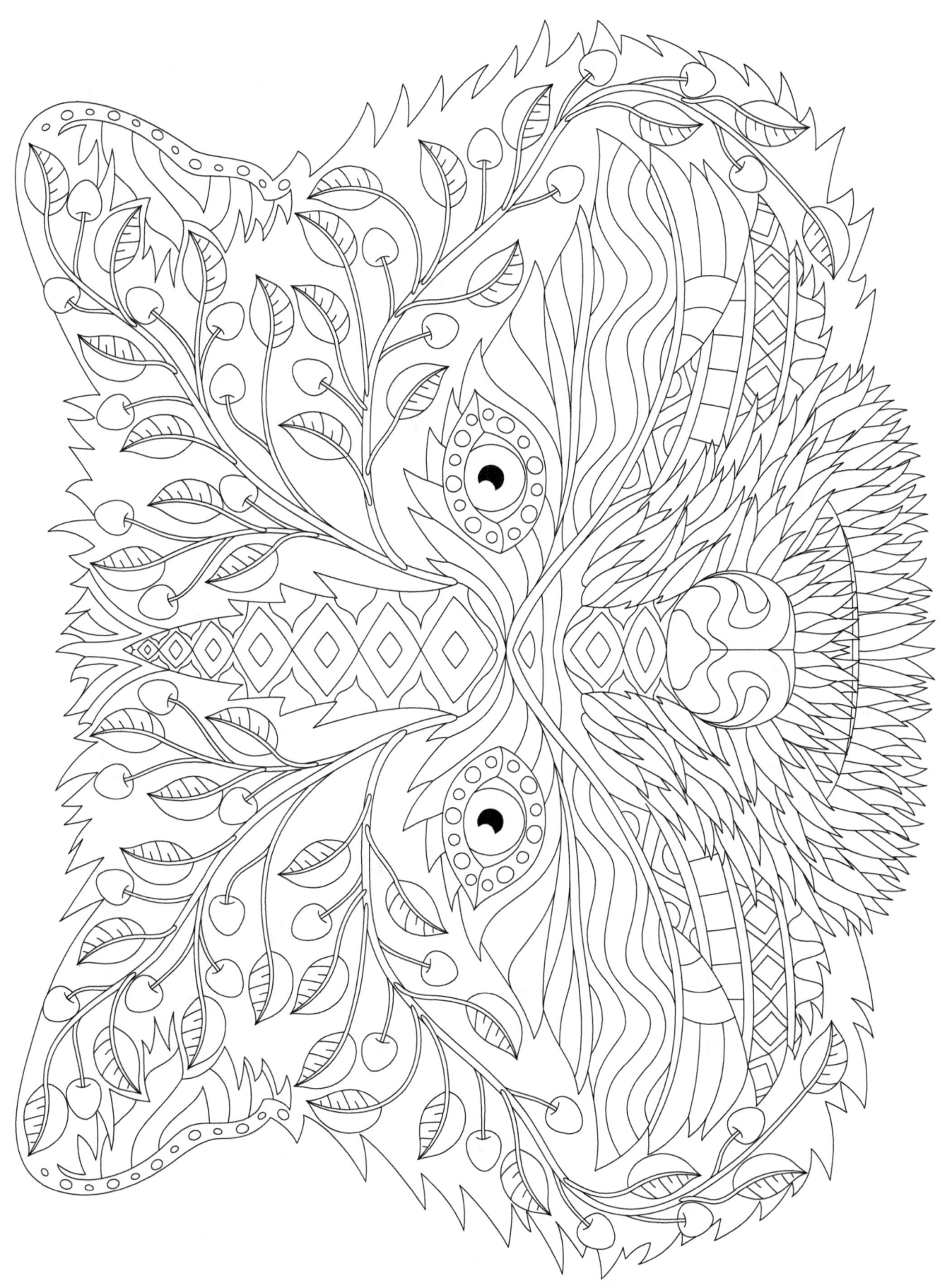

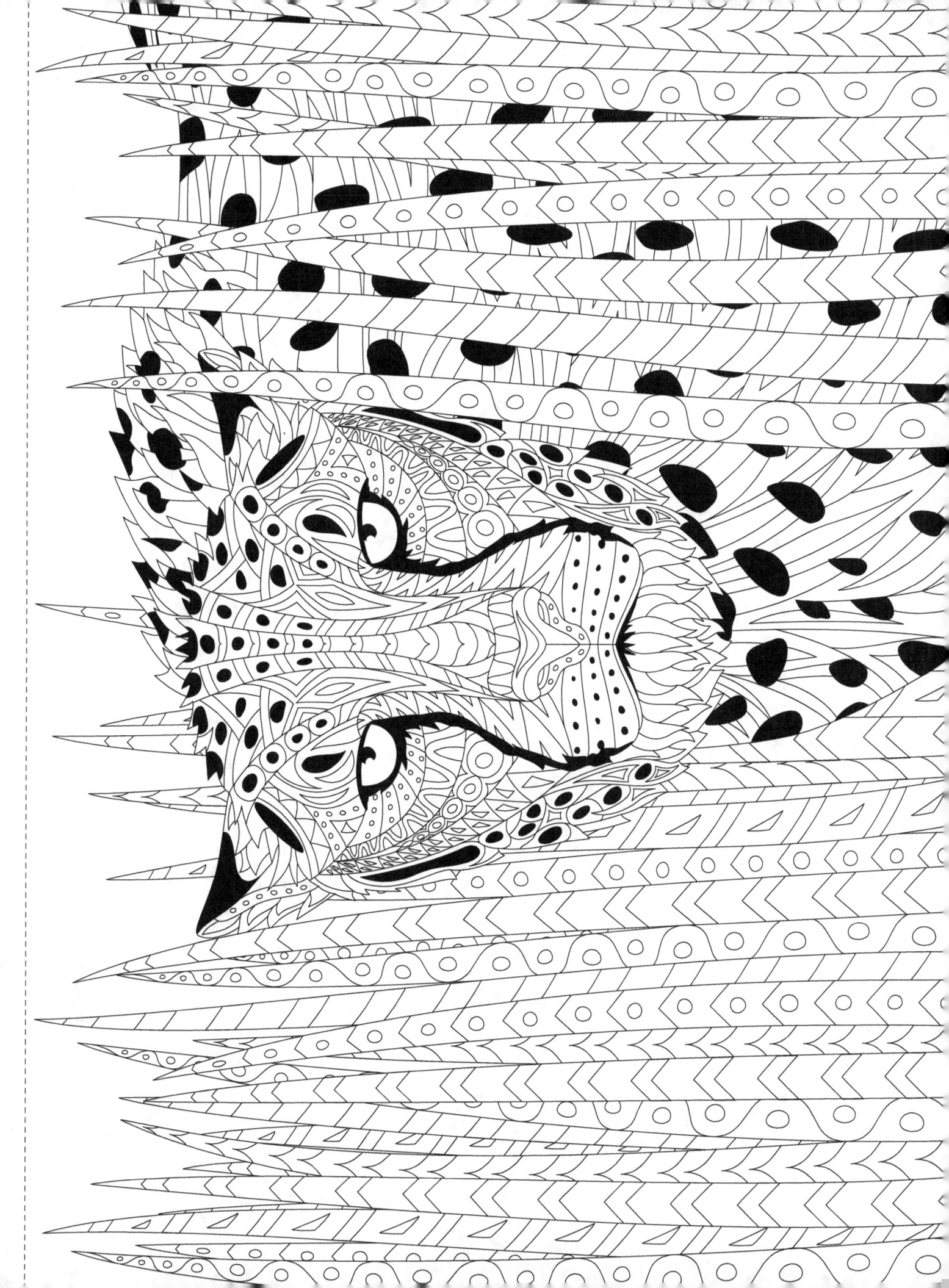

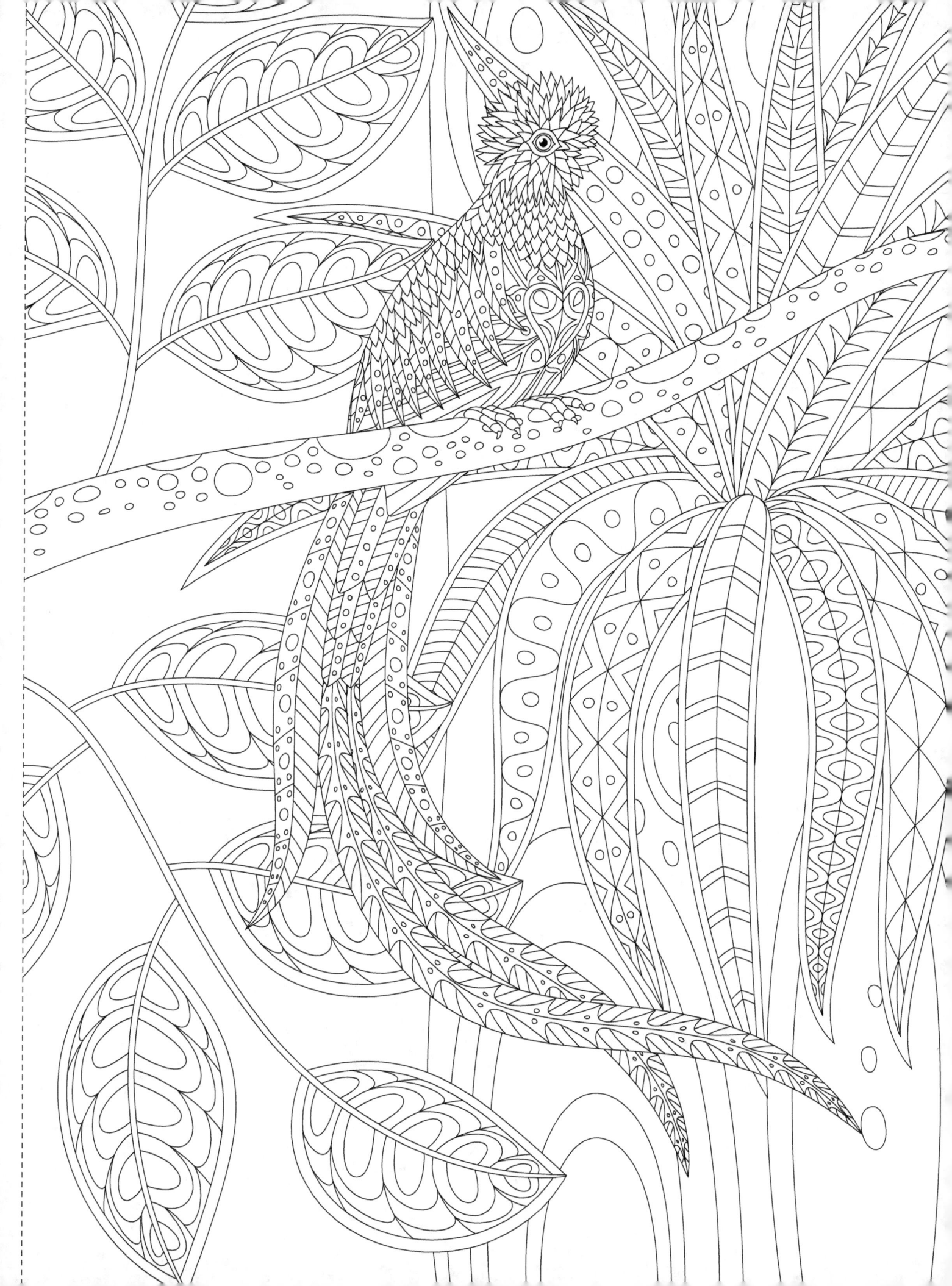

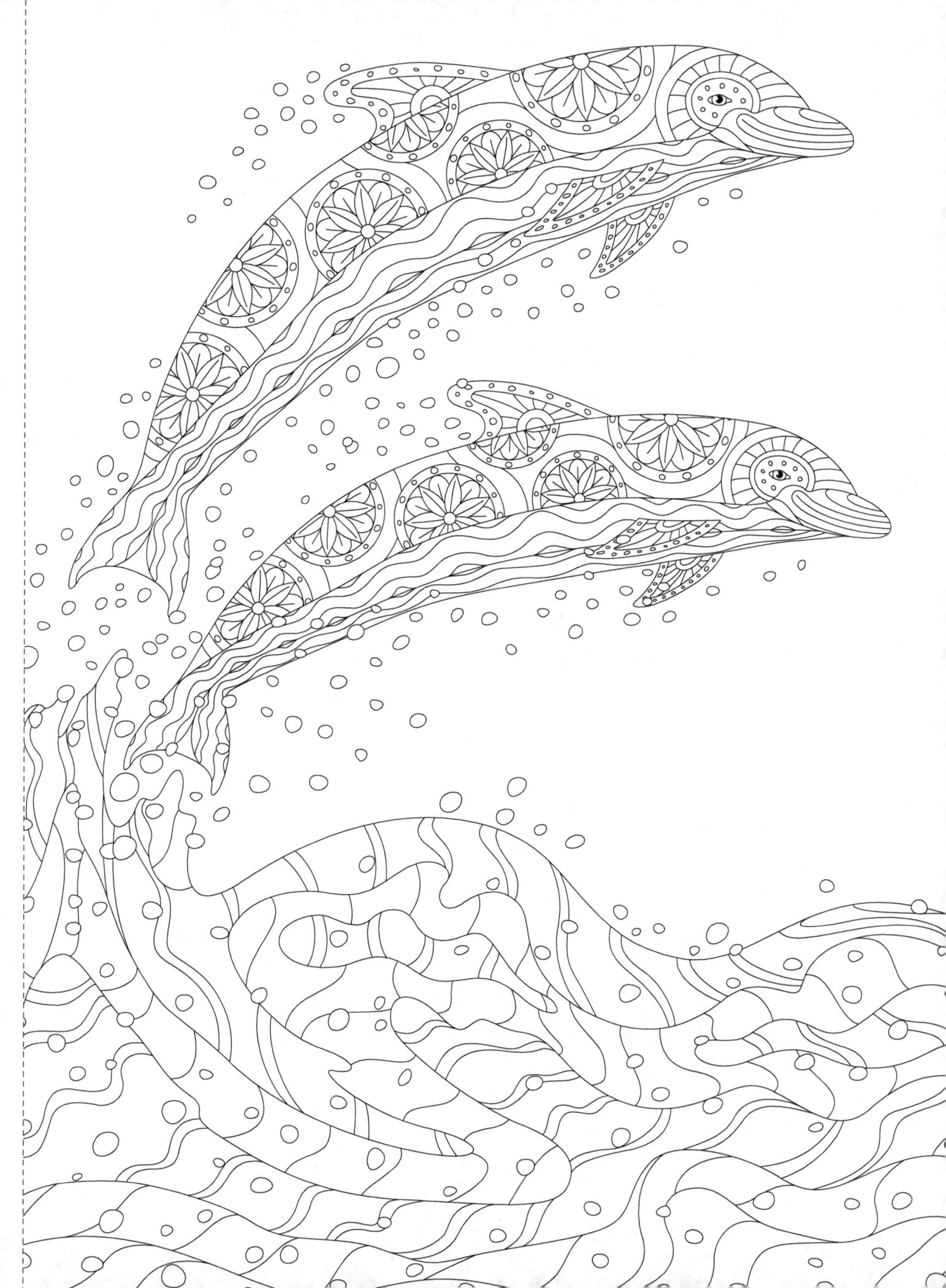

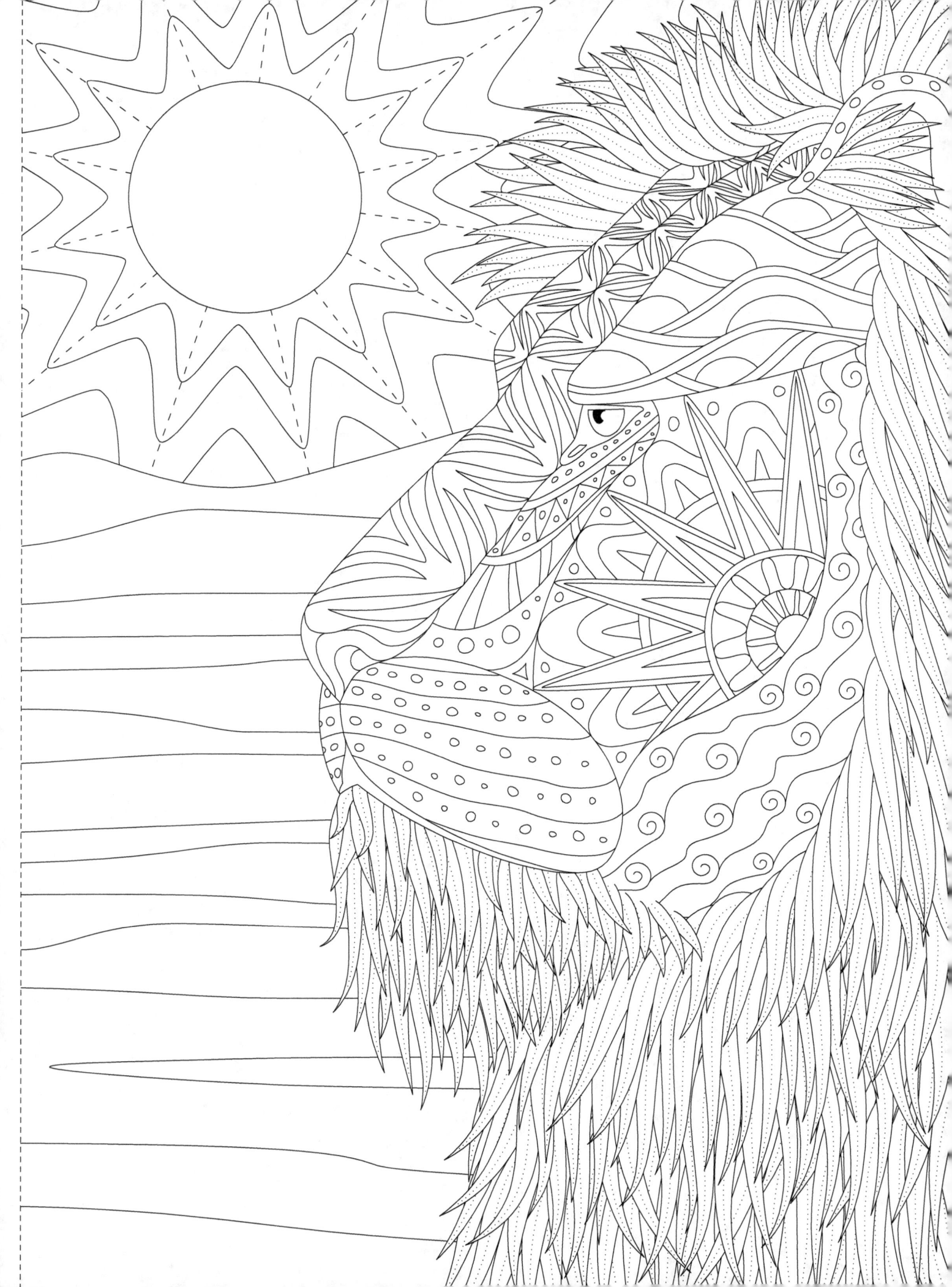

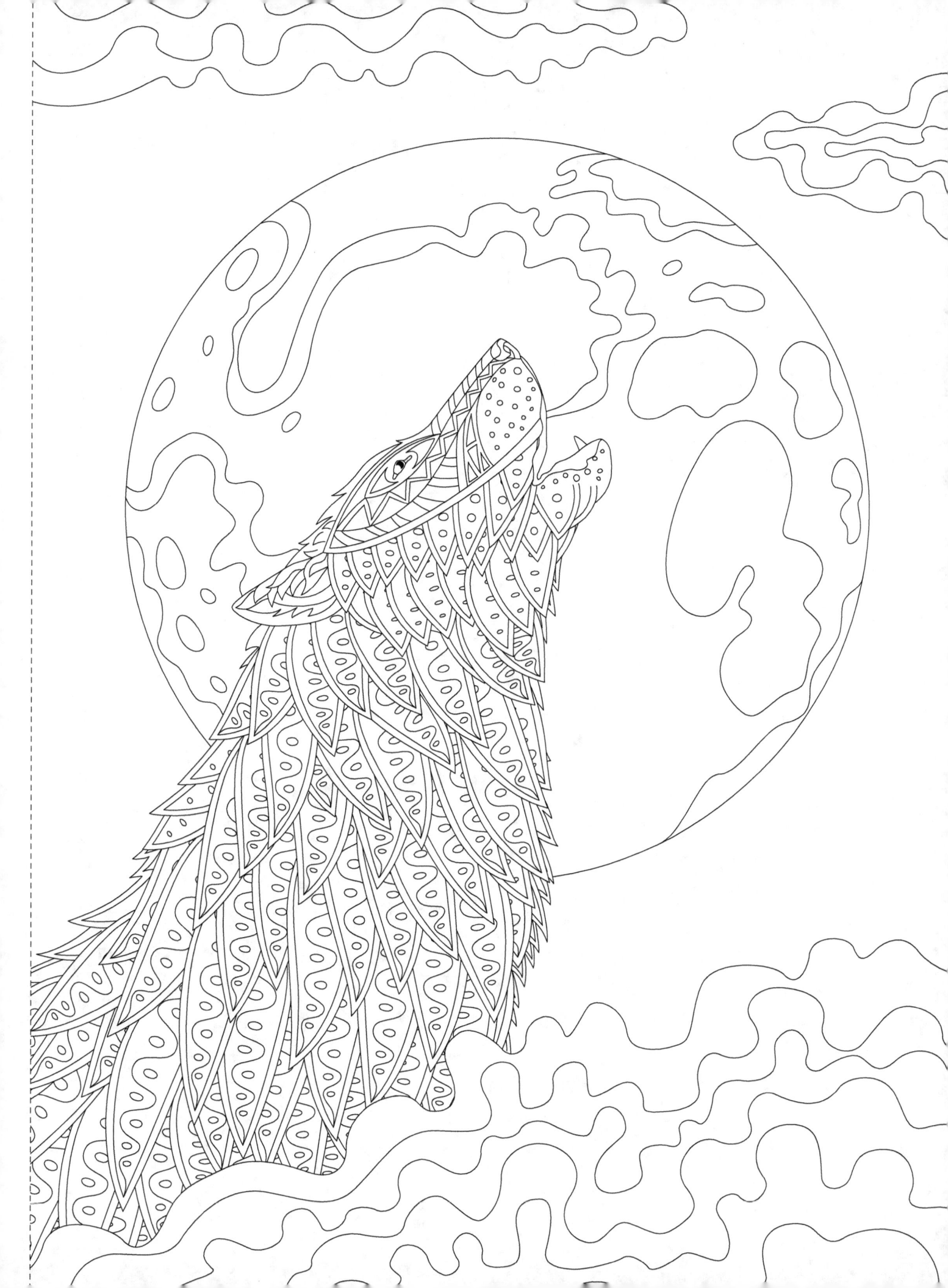

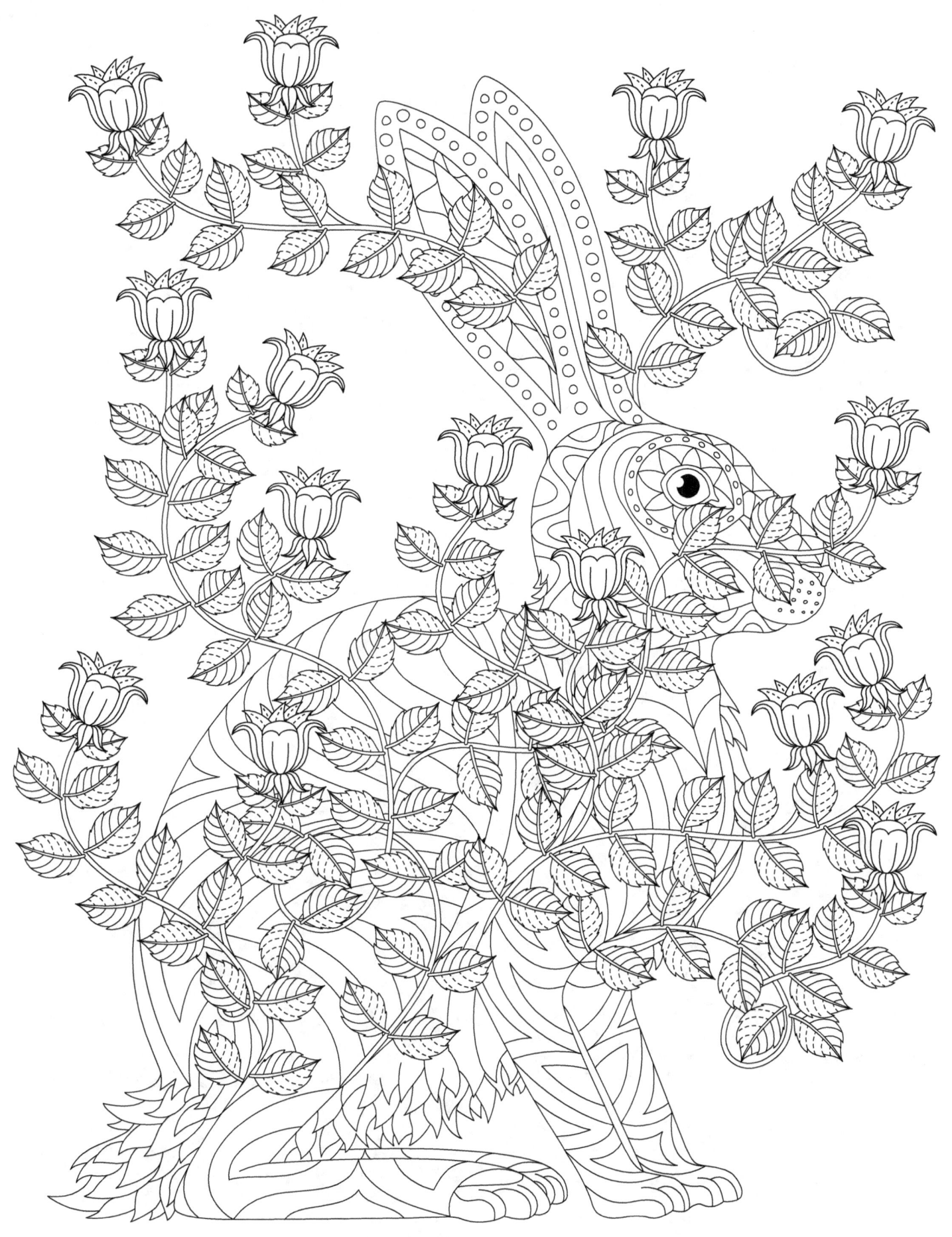

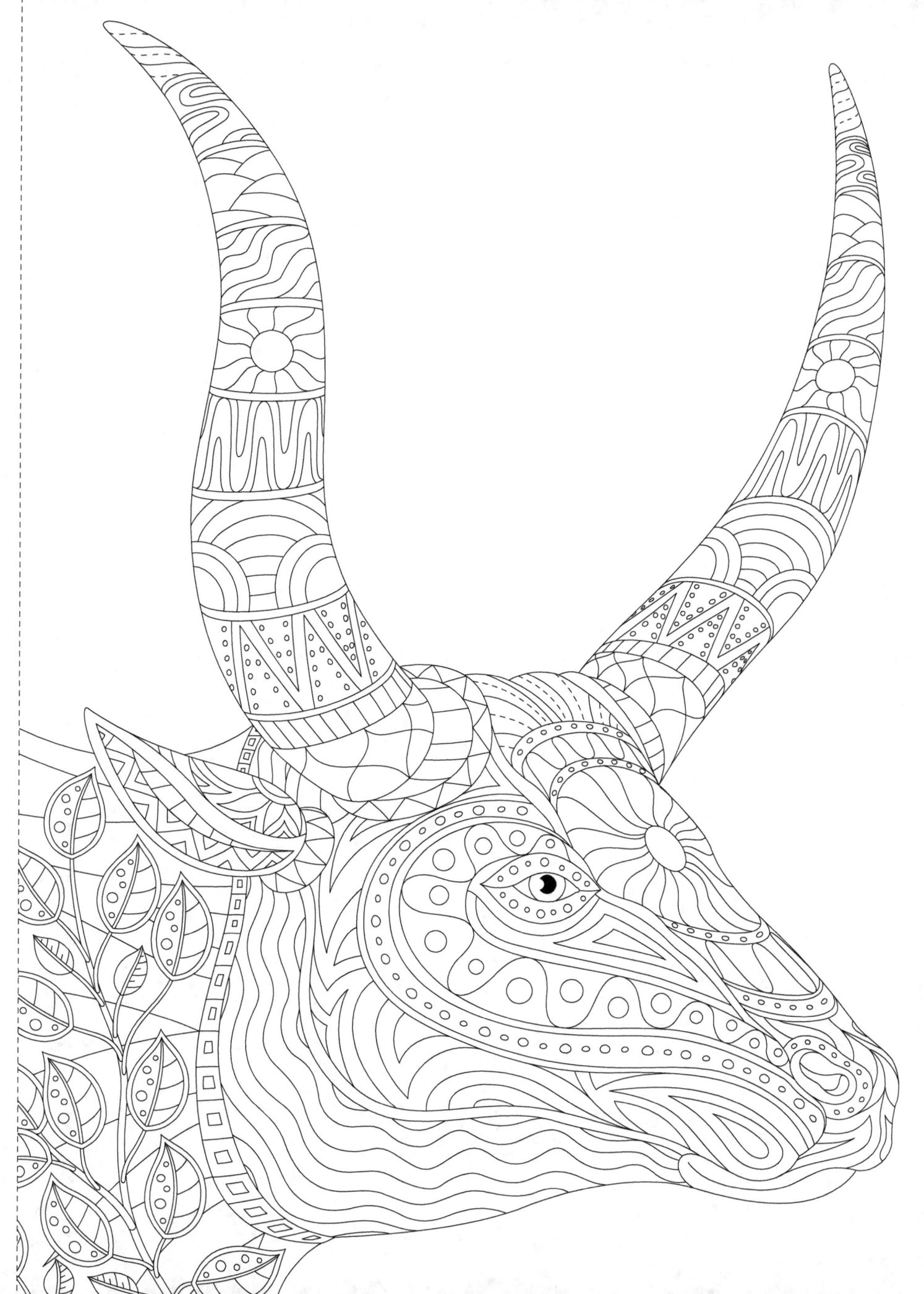

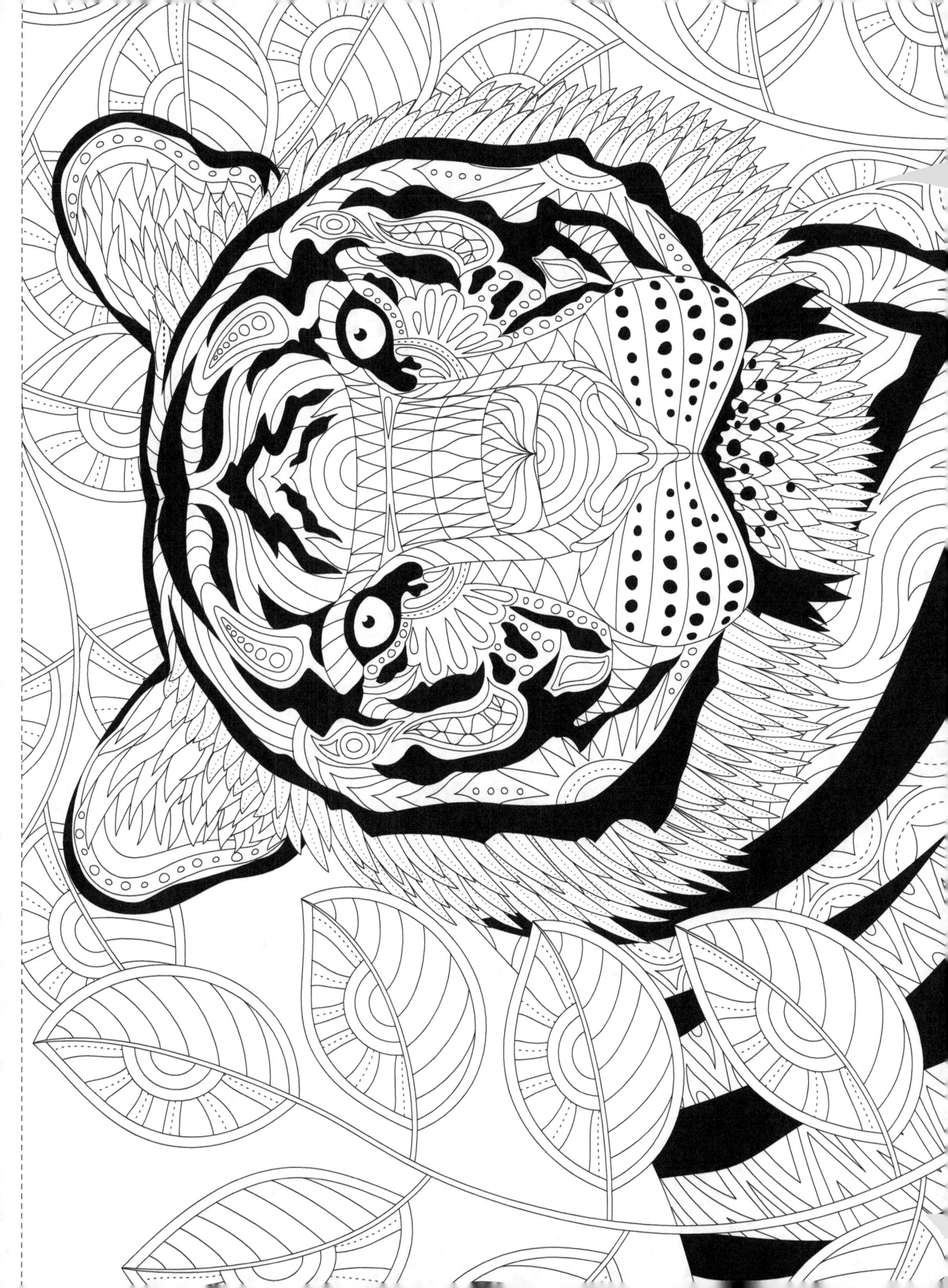

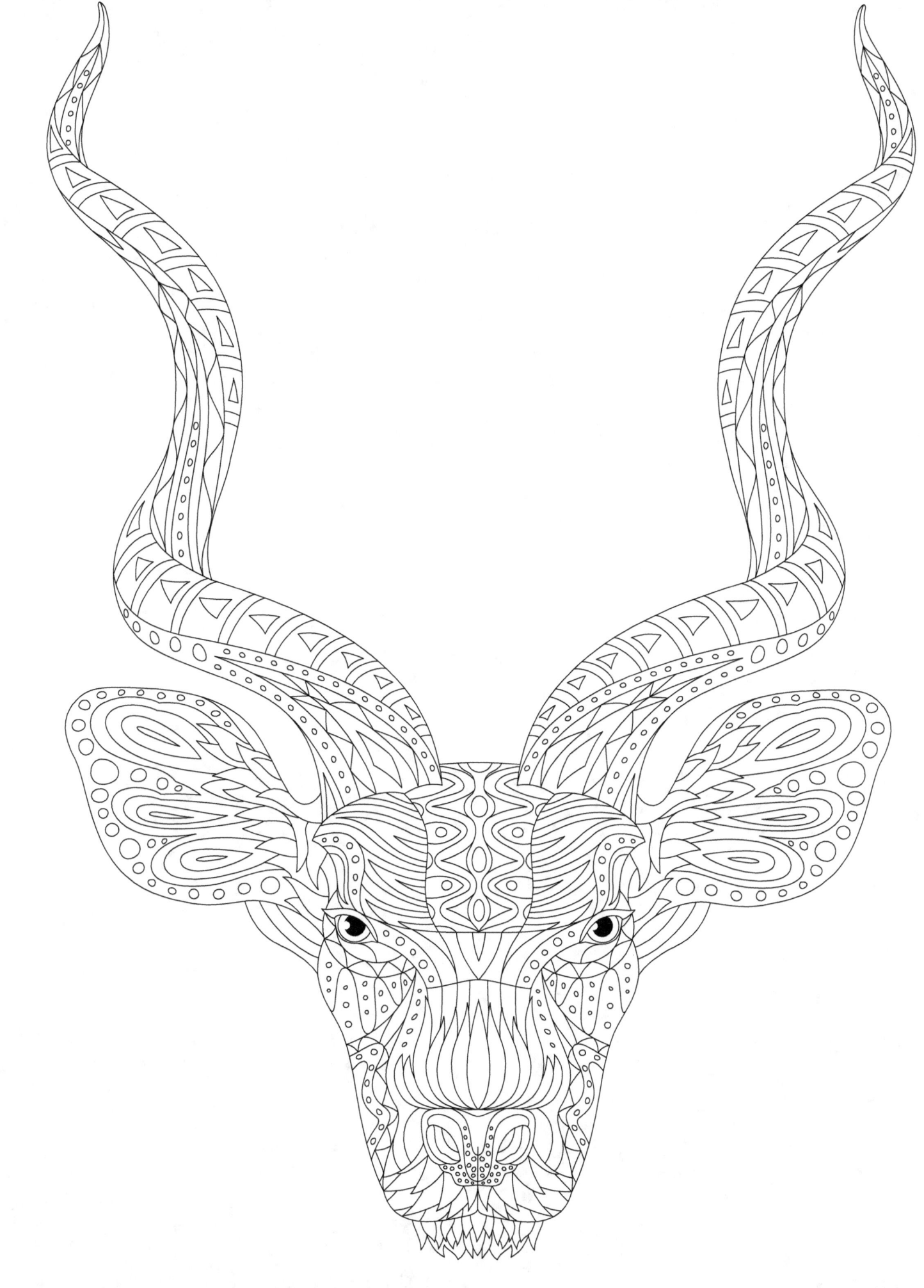

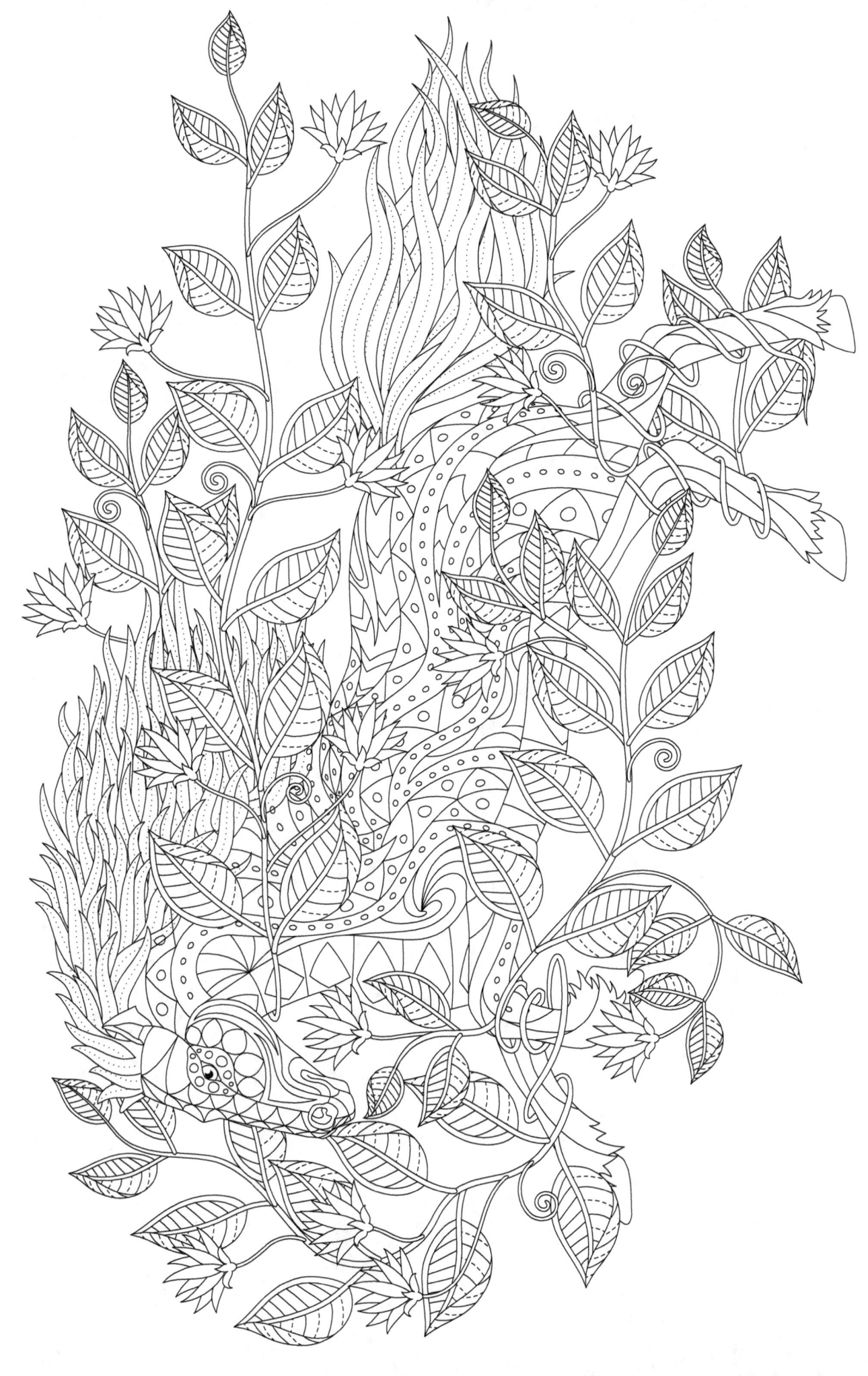

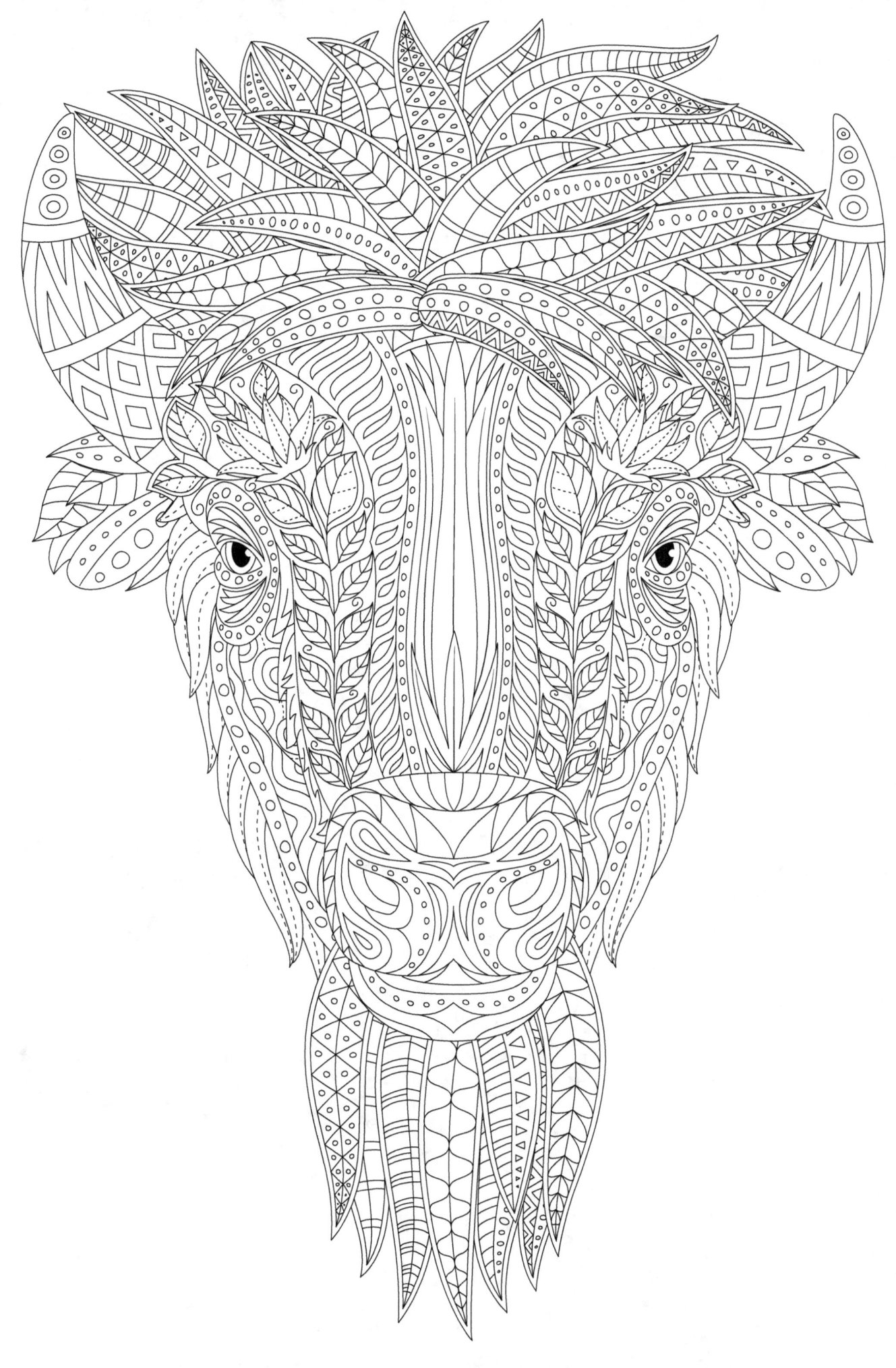

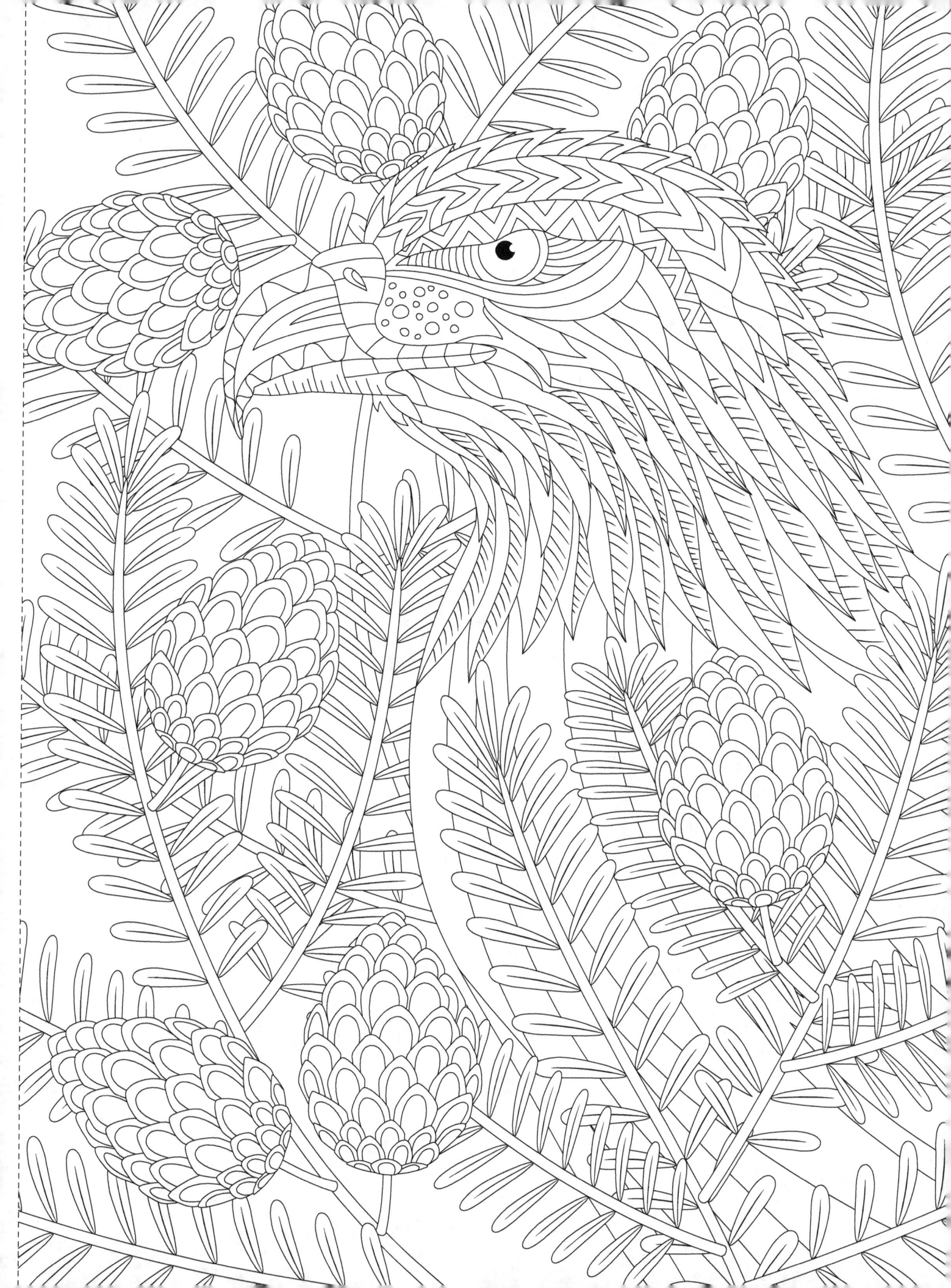

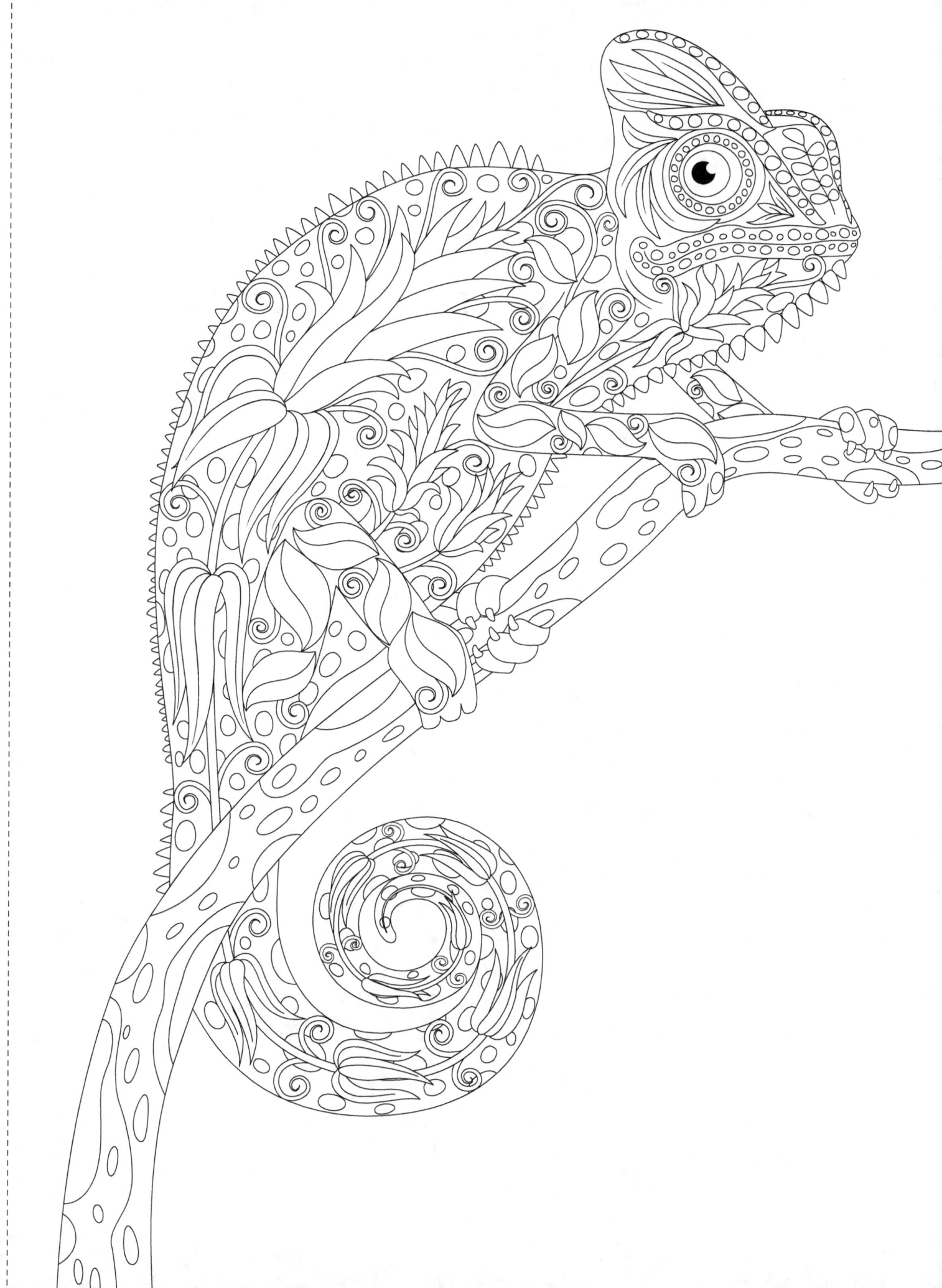

www.ingramcontent.com/pod-product-compliance
Lightning Source LLC
Chambersburg PA
CBHW081204180526
45170CB00006B/2208